D0014881

3

A
Boy
Named
Phyllis

A
Boy
Named
Phyllis

A SUBURBAN
MEMOIR

Frank DeCaro

Viking

VIKING
Published by the Penguin Group
Penguin Books USA Inc., 375 Hudson Street,
New York, New York 10014, U.S.A.
Penguin Books Ltd, 27 Wrights Lane,
London W8 5TZ, England
Penguin Books Australia Ltd, Ringwood,
Victoria, Australia
Penguin Books Canada Ltd, 10 Alcorn Avenue,
Toronto, Ontario, Canada M4V 3B2
Penguin Books (N.Z.) Ltd, 182–190 Wairau Road,
Auckland 10, New Zealand

Penguin Books Ltd, Registered Offices:
Harmondsworth, Middlesex, England

First published in 1996 by Viking Penguin,
a division of Penguin Books USA Inc.

1   3   5   7   9   10   8   6   4   2

Grateful acknowledgment is made for permission to reprint an
excerpt from "Curtains" by Elton John and Bernie Taupin. Used by
permission of Rocket Records.

LIBRARY OF CONGRESS CATALOGING-IN-PUBLICATION DATA
DeCaro, F. A.
A boy named Phyllis : a suburban memoir / by Frank DeCaro.
p.   cm.
ISBN 0-670-86718-7
1. DeCaro, F. A.—Childhood and youth.   2. Gay youth—New
Jersey—Biography.   3. New Jersey—Social life and customs.
4. Suburban life—New Jersey.   I. Title.
HQ75.8.D43A3   1996
305.2'35'08664—dc20   95-49082

This book is printed on acid-free paper.

∞

Printed in the United States of America
Set in Adobe Garamond
Designed by Jaye Zimet

To my mother and father,
Marian and Frank DeCaro,
without whom this book
would not have been possible
. . . or necessary.

Cultivate the freshest flower
This garden ever grew,
Beneath these branches
I once wrote such childish
words for you.
But that's okay.
There's treasure children
always seek to find,
And just like us
You must have had
A Once Upon A Time.
—FROM "CURTAINS," BY
ELTON JOHN AND
BERNIE TAUPIN

By the year 2000, half the
world will be crazy and the
other half will be queer.
—MARIAN DeCARO, 1972

Why must your life be an
open book?
—FRANK DeCARO, SR., 1980

Acknowledgments

These people were truly the wind beneath my wing tips during the writing of *A Boy Named Phyllis* and to them I give all my love and thanks: Harry Althaus, Erica Berger, Marian and Frank DeCaro, Joyce DiBonaventura-Famighetti, Don Fehr, Angela Miller, and Dan Weiller.

My heartfelt appreciation goes to Elton John and Gianni Versace, brave men who've shown me more kindness than I could ever possibly return, to Bernie Taupin for writing words to live by, and to Ed Filipowski for bringing *Phyllis* to Sharon.

Recognition also must go to Derek Anderson, Christine Baird, Carol Bennett, John Capouya, Leslie Cohn, Ken Fallin, Charles Flowers, Don Forst, Marisa Fox, Sharon Glassman, Michael Goff, Paige Greytok, Richard Hainey, Michael Hardart, Louise Harris, David Herndon, Chuck Hettinger, Alison Ilowite, Steve Isenberg, Tom Kulaga, Linnea Lannon, Heidi Lichtenstein, Marcy Hedy Lynn, David Messineo, Stanley Mieses, Susan Mulcahy, Denis O'Hare, Linda O'Keeffe, Ken Petronis, Sarah Pettit, Nancy

Plominski, Catharine Rambeau, Margaret Roach, Jackie Ross, Irene Sax, Barbara Schuler, Don Schwarz, James Sie, Phyllis Singer, Bruce Steele, Stanley Steinberg, Gene Sullivan, Scott Teagarden, Heidi Utz, Karen Van Rossem, and Susan Wyland for their encouragement, assistance, and unflagging support over the years.

And, finally, a belated thank-you to Frank Maya for telling me to put down the fork and pick up a pen.

Contents

A

Boy

Named

Phyllis

Miracle Baby

*I*t's safe to say, in my case, that it was not easy being a fetus.

On an April morning after a night of dancing the peabody with Booby Natale at the annual Bowling Banquet at Nestor's Inn—an oasis of sausage-and-pepper steam-tray swank in Singac, New Jersey—my mother, Marian Teresa LaRegina DeCaro, checked into Mount Sinai Hospital in Manhattan to have a large tumor removed. It was 1962; she was forty-three and believed she was unable to have children. When the surgeon, Dr. Salo Boltuch, extracted the melon-sized growth (they're *always* melon-sized) he found me behind it, desperate for attention. As memory serves, I looked up at the gentle-handed jamoke in the football-player-sized scrubs, waved hello, and said,

A
B o y
N a m e d
P h y l l i s

"Where the *hell* have you been?" I'd been there almost three months, waiting to be discovered.

I've always joked about being Marian and Frank DeCaro, Sr.'s, fourth miscarriage, and that morning I could very well have ended up in a bag marked MED-ICAL WASTE in a dumpster somewhere on 101st Street. Instead, a little more than six months later, I ended up in New Jersey. My arrival turned an Italian Catholic working-class couple into a threesome just in time for their eleventh wedding anniversary.

I made my debut at eight A.M. on Election Day via routine cesarean, which my mother was told would make for a more beautiful baby, one not so squashed. But my father didn't find out I'd been born until five hours later, even though he'd been in the hospital waiting room all morning. "Ooh, I forgot to tell Frank," Dr. Boltuch said, when my father's sister Angie called to find out how things went. He'd goofed again, but it didn't matter. Angie would break the news to my father.

She always knew everything first, anyway.

A woman with jet-black Priscilla Presley–as–Italian–widow hair and a penchant for leopard print, Angie was home that morning in New Jersey making spritz cookies and padding around the linoleum bare-foot with wet toenails and paper toweling between each red-lacquered digit so they wouldn't smudge. She had my father paged at Sinai, and when he finally came to the phone, pressing the receiver anxiously to his ear, she said: "It's a boy! Now bring that Miracle Baby home!" That's what my ever-dramatic, ever-outspoken godmother—the woman I most took after —called me: the Miracle Baby. But, as far as I can tell, the only thing truly miraculous about my birth was the location.

Thanks to my mother's honeydew of a tumor, I am a native New Yorker. It says so on my passport. But I didn't grow up "riding the subway, running with people, up in Harlem, down on Broadway" the way that disco song would have you believe. I grew up riding in a white Chrysler Newport, running with people who wouldn't have gone to Harlem if their lives depended on it. And as for Broadway—well, we were strictly theater party, let's–go–see–*A Chorus Line*–on–a–bus, and rear mezzanine at that. We were Jersey people, Marian, Frank Senior, and me, products of the aluminum-sided, lawn-sprinklered, what-exit? wilds of suburbia, genuine dyed-in-the-mall articles. Purple furniture you weren't allowed to sit on, four-foot above-ground swimming pool in the backyard, artificial Christmas tree, Ragú on Ronzoni . . . we had it all, and a two-car garage to boot.

New Jersey was all my parents knew. My bald-headed teddy-bear-cute father and my pear-shaped bundle of Aqua-Net mother were born and raised only a few minutes' drive from the house where I grew up. That's where they still live, and, like all parents of only children, maintain their son's bedroom as a shrine. My father and I even went to the same high school, the class of '40 and the class of '80. But, for me, my hometown of Little Falls was the place from which I most wanted to escape, once I saw that there was more to life than the Little Falls Lanes bowling alley, the Valley Spa luncheonette, and Sunday school at Holy Angels. I left as soon as I could—at seventeen, already an out-of-the-closet homosexual with one serious relationship under my Pierre Cardin, New Wave–skinny belt. But like everyone else who grew up there, I have a lifetime membership. New Jersey is like Catholicism and certain branches of Jack LaLanne—they never let you go.

I suppose there are worse things than growing up in a town that counts among its chief industries the manufacture of latex condoms. (It makes having safer sex feel like Old Home Week.) But Little Falls wasn't exactly the land of milk and hospitality for a young gay boy or, for that matter, anyone who felt different. A jumble of bi-levels and ranch houses—swing sets in backyards, Chevys out front—Little Falls was actually very cute as small towns go.

It was only twenty-five minutes and a world away from Manhattan.

I like to think of the eighteen miles between my childhood home and my adult apartment in the gay mecca of Chelsea as aesthetic distance. Kaleidoscopic diversity wasn't valued in Little Falls. Change was bad. In fact, to be anything but ordinary was a mistake. But I couldn't help myself. I was *born* gay. It just took sixteen years for me to figure it out. Unfortunately, the other children in the neighborhood realized my destiny a lot sooner.

Like a lot of major homosexuals-to-be, I spent much of my childhood being haunted by a handful of kids who made sissy-torture their life's work. They were enthusiastically malicious, stripping me (and every other different kid) of the self-esteem we might have had. But they didn't succeed completely. All they did was fuel my desire for escapism and, ultimately, escape.

When Little Falls proved inhospitable, I created my own world to play in. With my friend Heidi, who would turn out to be my first girlfriend, I let television and books and make-believe make up for all that was lacking, beyond the manicured front lawns, in the patchwork houses of our little town on the not-so-mighty Passaic River. Precocious together, we pretended as a way to smooth over the misfitting of our lives in suburbia, excelling at school and keeping each other supremely amused.

We learned what there was to learn in Little Falls in three elementary schools imaginatively called School #1, School #2, and School #3. There was one in each of the town's three neighborhoods—Great Notch, Singac, and Little Falls. We had a half-dozen churches sprinkled here and there, including ours, Holy Angels, where the pastor, a dashing Franciscan with a hint of a brogue, would call me handsome one week and then deliver a sermon on the evils of homosexuality and masturbation the next.

There was the high school, Passaic Valley, home of the Hornets. It was the place where I was most miserable and, for a few shining moments, happier than I'd ever been. There was an Entenmann's outlet that advertised in the church bulletin and where they knew repeat customers like my family by name; and a ShopRite supermarket so big the managers handed out maps after its last remodeling. Everyone from Passaic Valley worked there at one time or another. For fun, there was a sleigh-riding hill at the top of Third Avenue, and, at the bottom of First, a park with a giant Army tank up on blocks that we loved to climb on and play Vietnam War. On Main Street in the center of town, there was the Oxford Barber Shop, where Tommy Fazio would always call me Little Bucky— Frank Senior was Big Bucky—and then scare me with the noisy hand vacuum he used to suck the hair off. Across the street was Tony's Pizza, where if you held your slice with the point down, the grease would pour off by the bucketful. Next door was Stanton's Drugs, where Aunt Angie would deliver a plate of cherry winks wrapped in aluminum foil once every couple of weeks in the belief that well-fed druggists offered better service, and, near that, the Little Falls Savings and Loan, which we called Jack's Bank because our neighbor was the president.

In Singac, not far from where my mother and

Booby cut that prenatal rug, there was a ceramics studio, where in the 1970s Heidi and I painted zodiac plaques, listened to "Rock the Boat" on an old FM radio, and got high on spray fixative. And then there was Prospect Street—and our house, which was white with ivory-colored brick trim, black shutters, and a bright red door.

My live-in grandmother, Anna LaRegina, a four-foot-tall Italian woman who smelled like Chiclets and lavender perfume, was always sitting on the porch steps in WAC shoes, a floral-print muumuu, and a permanent tan, drinking Pabst Blue Ribbon and reading *The Love Machine.* With upper arms that hung like parade-float bunting, the constitution of a battleship, and the salty vocabulary of a sailor on shore leave, she was as much a fixture as the Blessed Virgin Mary statue that stood in front of the place in a bathtub-shaped plaster grotto.

My mother, her daughter, was born in Paterson in 1919 and grew up in Totowa borough. My grandfather, Carney LaRegina, was a fabric finisher in a dye house; Grandma, the former Anna Andiorio, was a winder in the mills that gave Paterson the name Silk City. Marian had a brother named Victor, fourteen months her senior, who had a hairy chest and a growl of a voice. Everyone called him Papa Vic. When my mother asked her brother to teach her to drive, he drove his car to the top of the steepest hill in the neighborhood, put it in park, got out, took his dog with him, and said "Go ahead. Drive." Fifty years later, my mother would still complain, "Can you believe he took his dog with him?"

Vic wasn't any good at school, but Marian was worse. The one time she knew the answer to a teacher's question, she had laryngitis.

"Put your arm down, Queenie, you can't talk anyway," her English teacher, Mr. Charney, said. He called her that because *La Regina* is Italian for "the queen." Marian, though, was more the exotic princess type with brown hair and dark, almond-shaped eyes that earned her the childhood nickname Chink. Her looks made her popular with the fellows and she never wanted for a boyfriend. As teens, Marian and her friends formed the TNT Club, which stood for Totowa's Nutsy Twerps. They once had a party for twenty people, and fed everyone for only $3. That was the one story we heard about them and we heard it a lot. But pictures of the TNT Club—faded black-and-whites of clean-cut kids of immigrant parents, mugging for the camera—make it look like they had fun growing up.

In her clique, Marian was always considered the fancy one. And, compared to the white-socks-with-suits crowd we called our relatives, she *was* fancy. After dropping out of high school, she used her unemployment checks to pay for beauty school. She became a beautician, eventually owning several salons and developing a weakness for faux Pucci-print dresses, auburn hair dye, and black convertibles with red leather interiors.

"Your mother always acted like she was rich," cousin Jeannie, the Florida divorcée and Virginia Graham look-alike, would say. "She used to intimidate the hell out of all of us." My mother said that's why my father married her. "He thought I had money. I fooled him."

My father was born in 1922 in Great Notch. Neither of his parents, Santo DeCaro and Mary Luzzi, could read or write. Santo, or Sam as they called him, was a spool carrier in the Beattie Carpet Mills not far from the center of town; then he went to work in a quarry until he developed emphysema. Mary, who raised three children, was a reeler at the carpet mill. None of the kids on that side of the family were very good students, either. But compared to his sister and brother, my father was the family scholar.

At least he showed up to class.

Allen Ginsberg's father was my father's English teacher at Paterson Central High School. Frank Senior used to take a bus there, because there was no high school in Little Falls until his senior year, when Passaic Valley High School opened. He began playing baseball that year, 1940, and wanted to be a professional but never made it. Before that he was a pin boy at the Little Falls Lanes. In 1942, as he was going on twenty, he was drafted and shipped off to Fort Dix, then to various training camps in Texas and Indiana. He spent eighteen months overseas in the 610th Tank Destroyer Battalion. On VE Day, he was in Czechoslovakia. "It was just another day," he'd say. One day wasn't like every other day, however. He received a letter from his sister Angie that, as he says, "shook the shit out of me." His mother had died of a cerebral hemorrhage at age forty-nine. The Red Cross refused to let him go home for services. "That turned me off the Red Cross for good," he would always say.

In February 1951, Marian and Frank were introduced by Jean Cosloy, one of my mother's customers at Marianne's, the beauty shop Marian co-owned in Paterson. She told my mother that she knew an eligible bachelor who worked for Curtiss-Wright, which made propellers, and asked if it would be okay if he called her. She said yes, and he did. On their first date, my father wore a gray suit, a charcoal overcoat, and a matching fedora, and picked up Marian LaRegina in a gunmetal-gray '46 Plymouth. Up until then, Frank had been dating a woman named Isabel, whose memory my parents would still debate forty-five years later.

"She was homely," my mother would say.

"Get the hell out of here, she was pretty!" my father would counter.

"She was fat!" Marian would maintain.

"She was a little heavy," my father would admit. "But she had a pretty face!"

It didn't matter what she was, because once my

parents met, Isabel was history. Marian and Frank went to the movies a lot, to dinners at Nestor's, and to an occasional hockey game in New York City. They were both good Italian Catholic kids, so they smooched a lot, but never got laid. They didn't believe in sex before marriage. To hear my father tell it many years later, my mother didn't believe in sex *after* marriage, either. "I married a nun," he'd say. "None today, none last night . . ." It was one of his running jokes.

On November 25, 1951, nine months after they met, Marian and Frank were married at St. James Roman Catholic Church in Totowa by the Reverend Francis J. Reilley. She wore a blush satin gown with a Queen Anne collar and a lace-paneled full skirt with a nine-foot train, and carried an orchid and a satin-covered prayer book in her hands as she made her way down the aisle. Aunt Angie was matron of honor in a strapless gown of American Beauty taffeta with a velvet bodice and a matching cocktail jacket. Papa Vic was best man. Bridesmaids wore emerald-green taffeta. The reception was for two hundred people at a nearby hall called Morningside. There was a buffet, which cost them $2.75 a head, and everyone was happy, eating and dancing a fox-trot, a peabody, and as the affair wore on a tarantella, which was my grandmother's specialty. As gifts, some people gave $3 in an envelope, others $5 and $10. The guy who managed my father's baseball team gave the new couple $25, which was so extravagant, they couldn't believe it. No one had that kind of money to give away so freely.

Marian and Frank went on a road trip to Washington, D.C., for their honeymoon and then, with my grandmother Anna, moved into a white ranch house on Lincoln Avenue in Pompton Plains. For a decade, they lived there, all three, more or less together. They always wanted to make it four and, despite my father's jokes about no sex after marriage, tried desperately. But Marian and Frank remained childless. Until Little Frankie—"Franconino," as Stepgrandma Carmela, who didn't speak English, called me—entered their lives that November in 1962. Before my first birthday, we moved to Prospect Street in Little Falls—three Italians and the future boy named Phyllis.

Then the fun *really* began.

**A t
H o m e
w i t h t h e
M u n s t e r s**

*B*eyond the red door
of our house on Prospect Street, and up a flight of
stairs covered in mauve sculptured carpeting—a floor
fashion that beautifully complemented the purple
down-filled loveseat and gilt cherub-head side tables
in our not-to-be-lived-in living room—past the white
Formica-topped counters, and across the pebbled linoleum of the kitchen floor was the room we called
the porch. It was supposed to be one, but Pete Par-
dine, who built our house, convinced Frank Senior
during construction to make it an enclosed sunroom
instead. It was a good idea. From the day we moved
in, my family spent its "quality" time in that room
alone.

It was on the porch, with its wood-paneled walls
and its plaid Herculon couch, that I ran around in

13

A
B o y
N a m e d
P h y l l i s

footy pajamas, ate boiled-ham sandwiches with lettuce and tomato on Wonder Bread—Fleischmann's margarine on the ham side, Hellmann's mayonnaise on the other—and played with Buddy, the beagle puppy my parents got me, but a few months later gave to Uncle Tony in Paterson because, as my grandmother said, "That dog is too stupid to live here." Mostly, though, we spent our time on the porch because that's where we kept the TV, even though it was the brightest room in the house. We rarely, if ever, turned off that old black-and-white Zenith. It brought us together, as it brought us the world.

Well, actually, it brought us *Hollywood Squares* and *The Mike Douglas Show;* Ed Sullivan and Topo Gigio on Sunday nights; and a situation comedy that reminded me of the average American family into which I'd been born: *The Munsters.*

Most kids lived their childhood lives as if they were episodes of *Leave It to Beaver* or *The Brady Bunch,* but I was convinced that my family was the Munsters, lovably monstrous creatures straight off the Universal back lot, kin to Boris Karloff and Bela Lugosi. To me, the goings-on at 1313 Mockingbird Lane, where this clan of Transylvanian transplants lived in a decrepit mansion with a fire-breathing dragon under the stairs, were like DeCaro home movies. They were a Borscht Belt version of the Addams Family, and so were we . . . even if we were Italian and only Esther, the crossing guard's daughter, thought our house was a mansion.

In my mind, Frank and Marian were Herman and Lily Munster, look-alikes for Frankenstein and Vampira; my grandmother was Count Dracula in a housedress. I was cast—by default—as Eddie Munster, the pointy-eared were-kid with fangs and a Little Lord Fauntleroy suit. But I felt more like Marilyn, the family's ugly duckling cousin. This unfortunate girl, golden-haired, with delicate features, was the blond sheep of the family—totally unlike her relatives, but bound to them nonetheless. She was Marilyn Munster even if she looked like Marilyn Monroe.

The Munsters were a strange family, to be sure, with a mad scientist's laboratory in the basement and an upright coffin in the hallway serving as a satin-lined phone booth. But they thought they were completely normal. It was *other* people who were weird, who didn't have it quite as good as they did. We felt *exactly* the same way. Other people were deprived. We had it all. And, at the time, it seemed like we did.

In the world I knew, no one led a life more posh than ours. Certainly not our next-door neighbors. Justine, the dirty little girl who lived over the fence when we first moved in, used to drape raw bacon over the handlebars of her tricycle so it'd be there whenever she wanted a between-meals snack. Her mother was too busy trying to break into show business to cook breakfast for her. Certainly our relatives didn't have a smidgen of the off-the-wall-to-wall luxury I took for granted.

Papa Vic and his family had each other, but not much else. A fireman and a part-time carpenter, he would show up on holidays with his wife, Marie, and their five children—four girls and a boy—all in hand-me-downs, although where the boy's hand-me-downs came from no one knew. They lived in the house my mother was raised in, a block from the church in which my parents were married, in a town whose only claim to fame was a bakery that made the best mutton pies in the state.

Their ramshackle house in Totowa was only five miles from our suburban dream home, but in it they lived as if they were in the country. Papa Vic shot deer. Aunt Marie put up preserves and tended to their dogs, a black-and-white beagle named Ace (Buddy's brother, in fact) and a poodle named Socks, whom my grandmother called Shotsy, just because she liked that name better. They kept ducks, too, and ate scrambled duck eggs for breakfast at a mess-hall-style table with benches for seats. They were earthy and resourceful, and did everything for themselves but make their own penicillin.

On my father's side were Uncle Charlie and Aunt Helen, who lived in a tiny old gray-and-white house in Haledon. He was a lovable slob who said "sang-wich" instead of "sandwich" and whose thick-and-thins always had holes in them, which we noticed whenever he took off his shoes. Felix to his Oscar, she was so compulsive she would weigh her meatballs and measure the silver tinsel garland on her Christmas tree so it would hang evenly all the way around. Charlie had been a bookie, a dishwasher, and a bowling alley pin boy. Helen was a homemaker who lived to smoke and to sip rye-and-ginger. She was a real dame—although not a floozy—who fell for Charlie in his bookmaking salad days, when, as my father said, "he pissed away more money than most people would ever see." He lost it the same way he made it—gambling. A few years before Uncle Charlie's death, when he found out his favorite nephew was gay, he said, "It must have come from his mother's side. We don't have that on our side of the family." And, as far as I could tell, they didn't. Except for one cousin who married a man and divorced him two weeks later and then moved in with a woman in Florida. No one ever talked about her.

Not even Aunt Angie, and she talked about everyone.

My father's sister, Angie, had an outgoing nature that was matched only by her love of gossip and her sense of mischief. Much to my mother's dismay, Angie and I were two of a kind. "If I'd known you were going to take after her, I wouldn't have let her be your godmother," Marian would say. Angie had had a miscarriage a few years before I was born, and my arrival helped her get over the loss she felt. Although she had two sons of her own—each celebrated with a wall of framed eight-by-ten photos in his bedroom—Angie treated me like I was her own, keeping me at her house for hours at a time, and schlepping me with her wherever she went. I was her kiddie companion once her kids became teenagers.

Angie was friends with everyone in Little Falls, making the rounds in a beat-up Chevy. She could schmooze better than anyone on either side of the family. Besides bringing cookies to the pharmacist at Stanton's Drugs, she'd bring spaghetti to Art Nigra, the gas station attendant, bread to Dr. Harvey, and sour cream streusel cake to the pastor at Holy Angels. Even from priests, she thought you got better service if you greased a few palms, or at least a few pans. She probably did.

At home, dressed in polyester shorts, print shell tops, and flip-flops, she'd cook and bake to her heart's content while playing a worn-out copy of "These Boots Are Made for Walking," by Nancy Sinatra. It was one of her favorite records, and mine. The first time she slipped that 45 on her Motorola record changer, I was in ecstasy, enraptured by this Italian girl from the other side of the tracks. In Nancy's voice I heard the call of "glamour" for the first time, right there on the linoleum in front of Angie's side-by-side refrigerator.

I would dance the pony, double-timing each step, arms close, hands sticking out at my sides, palms to the floor. With dark brown hair, brown eyes rimmed by the longest eyelashes any "tumor" had ever grown, and a lithe little body that had not yet grown fat, I was Frankie-a-Go-Go. A nancy boy in a plain white T-shirt and khakis, with a Batman iron-on on my thigh, I did the swim, holding my nose as I wiggled to the floor, while Angie made tunnel-of-fudge bundt cakes in a stand-up mixer, a telephone receiver on her shoulder, its long, long cord trailing on the floor behind her.

She was forever on the dish.

Impetuous and impatient, Angie would decide she wanted something and had to have it right then. What she craved most were shoes and handbags. Her hot-headed husband, Joe, used to say, "Yeah, Ange, that's what you need . . . another goddamned pair of shoes. You don't have enough." And then he'd run and open all her closet doors and dozens of pairs would fall out, cheap but in every color. "Don't you yell at me or I'll go buy more," Angie would say. And she would, too, whether he screamed at her or not.

When Angie and Joe retired to Florida, Joe's picture sometimes made one of the local papers because he'd caught a big fish. Angie would put a quarter in the honor box and steal a dozen copies to mail home to New Jersey. Joe caught her doing this once and scolded her: "What are you, nuts? Don't take all the papers out of one box!" So she never did again. "I promised I wouldn't," she explained. "So now I go to

At
Home
with the
Munsters

19

the box in front of Zayre's and take six copies, and then I go to the one in front of Piggly Wiggly and take six more."

Angie would drop information into conversations —"The woman across the street isn't speaking to me," for instance; if you asked why, she'd say she didn't know. But if you pressed her, she'd tell you.

"I called her daughter a slut," Angie would admit.

"No wonder she's not speaking to you," my mother would say.

Angie always felt that if something was the truth, you could say it and get away with it. I always agreed, telling everything I knew to anyone who'd listen. It was Angie's way of making sense of the world and, when I grew up, mine, too. In storytelling, she found salvation from the doldrums of suburbia. Her letters from Florida brimmed with self-importance— drugstore greetings filled with news and punctuated with "(Ha! Ha!)"'s.

Angie's loose tongue and poison pen were given a run for their money only by my grandmother Anna, who lived in the ground-floor studio apartment in our house among crocheted-poodle bottle covers, book-cases of Reader's Digest Condensed Books, and a stand-up roaster that produced the most perfect chicken and potatoes outside of Naples. She was a pistol.

Her room was paneled in unidentifiable brown wood the color of Baker's chocolate when you leave it in the vegetable drawer of the refrigerator too long. The floor was a checkerboard of linoleum on top of concrete that was cool and damp even on the hottest day of summer, a fact to which Grandma attributed her constant arthritis. There was a white brick fireplace in her apartment, a fifties Formica-topped kitchen table upon which batches of Italian round cookies were rolled every Christmas, four heavy chairs upholstered in petrol blue vinyl, and a big off-white Kelvinator refrigerator, polished to a shine each week with Jubilee and a cut-up T-shirt.

The fridge had one floral decal stuck on it—Grandma's idea of personalization—and a stash of beer always inside, rows of gold-labeled bottles standing at attention behind glass keeper doors. Each afternoon, Grandma would open a bottle of her favorite brew using a "Fabulous Las Vegas Strip" opener, pour the amber contents into a Pilsner beer glass etched with polka dots, take a sip, and with an ear-wide grin utter a breathy "Aaaaaaaaaah!" that started at her toes. It was her signature.

We called her Nana, because it rhymed with Anna. She called me "Keecheepoopoonana." She lived in a world with its own language, Nana Anna, and a lot of it was naughty. There was one day when she got so mad at me, she told me "Go plug a dog!" I think I was about ten. Her Italian was equally inventive. Whenever someone asked Nana when she was going to bury the hatchet with her estranged sister, she

A t
H o m e
w i t h   t h e
M u n s t e r s

21

wouldn't say never. Instead, Nana would respond "Quando piscia gallina!," or "When a chicken pees." (She explained to me once that chickens don't pee.) My aunt Marie forbade her from using that expression in front of her children. Nana called me aside after they left that day, and said, "You can't have any fun with your cousins." With me, however, she could do or say anything. And did. When I was a child she would count on my toes: "Uno, due, tre, cazzo in culo a te"—which, roughly translated, means "One, two, three, a dick in your ass."

She knew something was up, even then.

As a baby-sitter, Nana was all any little boy could want. She was permissive and playful, an enthralling Old World spirit, with a deck of cards and a bag of knitting supplies always close at hand. She made our time together seem as much fun for her as it was for me. For hours on end, we would play rummy or do cat's cradle or just watch wrestling on TV. When my parents argued, making a racket during a match, she'd turn to them, say, "Would you shut the hell up, I can't hear them fall," and then turn back to the set and pull me close, my head nestled on one of her big droopy upper arms. We were an army of two in cahoots against them.

Most every day, Nana would wear a strand of blue pop beads, the kind you could fasten and unfasten for hours without getting bored, and sundresses that she'd

sewn on an old brushed-steel sewing machine. In the
'70s, she discovered polyester doubleknit pantsuits in
white or salmon, and she and my mother would bring
them home from an outlet store called Knit Studios
like they were Dior couture. She was a brown-eyed
vision with coarsely beautiful white hair, gelled a bit
with Alberto VO5 and given a bluish cast by White
Minx, a rinse that came in a silver-gray plastic bottle.
My mother would administer it whenever a hint of
yellow began to show. It didn't stink like the
permanent-wave solutions my mother used to curl her
hair, but it was mysterious to me nonetheless, part of
the beauty culture that informed my earliest years and
tied me to these two women.

Although Marian had closed her salon, Marianne's,
in Paterson years before I was born, and gave up her
chair at a salon called Frank's when I was in kindergarten, she kept her beauty operator's license until she
was in her sixties and always did Nana's hair at home.
On those days, we'd dig out a tarnished chrome hair
dryer, a monster of a thing with a dome as big as a
hatbox and twice as deep, from the storage room in
back of our garage. Elsa Lanchester could have fitted
her whole *Bride of Frankenstein* 'do under there. I always liked to stick my entire head in it, hair drenched
from a dunk in our backyard swimming pool, and
pretend I was caught in a tornado. Oh, the styles you
could create doing that! Nana, though, opted for a

A
B o y
N a m e d
P h y l l i s

simple wash and set that left her with a modified bouffant—cotton candy, but only a small portion. It was her look.

Under the dryer, she would read the trashiest novels: *Valley of the Dolls, Once Is Not Enough, The Moneychangers, The Carpetbaggers, Airport.* She loved a good potboiler. Sometimes you could spot her reading *Saints to Know and Love* under there—to keep us guessing—but usually it was Jacqueline Susann or Harold Robbins. When she was outside gardening, one of her favorite pastimes, I would sneak into her room and look through her books for the dirty parts. One of them had a scene in which a Middle Eastern lover spread cocaine on a woman's nipples and then roared into her like a juggernaut. That page kept me going for a week and a half. Once, Nana brought home from the remainders pile at Woolworth's a novel about the Mafia which had a particularly graphic description of oral sex in it. This don was getting the service of his life. She caught me reading it, noticed I had worked up a little-boy boner, and furiously threw the book in the fireplace. Grandma hated boners as much as she loved those novels.

It was no wonder why.

Nana's husband, Carney, had broken her heart by cheating on her with her sister Rosie—a woman who would forever be referred to as "the *whooor*" in our family. Nana never had much use for men after that.

She didn't have much use for women, either. She would instruct me, "Frankie, stay away from girls," never realizing the power of her words.

Carney and Rosie had made life miserable for Nana, carrying on in plain sight. Many a night, Rosie would come to their house in Totowa and, from the front porch, shout to Carney: "Is she dead yet?" And then they'd go out. Nana never forgave them, or men in general, even after her divorce. When I was a kid, she told me Grandpa was dead. And he was—but she'd been saying that for years before they planted him in Laurel Grove. She never let any of her older grandchildren get to know him either. Nana outlived both Carney and Rosie, a fact that pleased her no end. She relished a joke about a man who died making love to a prostitute: when rigor mortis set in, he had such an erection that the undertaker couldn't close the coffin. He called the wife and asked what she wanted him to do. "Cut it off and shove it up his ass," the wife replied. "Many a time he tried to do it to me."

The name LaRegina—"The Queen"—suited Nana better than her maiden name of Andiorio because, no matter how wonderful she was to her little Frankie, she could be a royal pain in the ass to my parents. To me she was an accomplice. But to them she was a permanent chaperone. In fact, the only trip they ever took without her was their honeymoon, and she wanted to go on that one, too. My father used to say,

A
B o y
N a m e d
P h y l l i s

"I've been married fifty years—twenty-five to your mother and twenty-five to your grandmother!" This wasn't far from the truth.

Frank Senior was defenseless against Nana's invincible will and her desire to be included in everything. Feeling tremendous loss over the premature death of his own mother, and, thanks to the Red Cross, denied even a sense of closure, he let his mother-in-law walk all over him. He would never put a stop to Nana's shenanigans. He couldn't talk back to a mother, even if she wasn't his. Before I was born, if Nana got mad at Marian or Frank, she would get "half in the bag," as my father put it, and run away from home. He'd have to get in the DeSoto and go up and down the streets looking for her and then beg her to come home. She always would, of course, knowing she could get away with murder if she wanted to.

For me, Nana made magic, telling me I was her favorite and making me believe it. Submerged in the mismatched cushions of her favorite chair, her thick ankles in rolled stockings propped up on an oblong footstool, she would hold me close while we watched *Dark Shadows* or *Voyage to the Bottom of the Sea* in color on her nineteen-inch RCA console. She lived for vampire stuff and loved underwater adventures. I was scared of Barnabas Collins's pointed teeth, but in love with David Hedison, especially when he put on a wetsuit. I would always move closer to the set to get a better look at his manliness, not yet knowing that the stirring I felt for him—from the top of his black-haired head to the bottoms of his flippered feet—was something of which the Catholic Church roundly disapproved.

Nana was *very* Catholic, but she never went to church. Near her bed, with its pastel-pink chenille spread, there was a hope chest that she used as an altar. Atop it was a chorus of saintly figures, hearts bleeding, crowns on straight, palms turned toward heaven, lit now and then by a votive candle. Here, she would pray for an ache or pain to go away, or for a winning entry in the Publishers' Clearing House sweepstakes. Every Sunday morning, amid her own personal Jesuses, Grandma would watch mass on TV. Once in a while, the deacon, Frankie Muoio from down the street, would come and give her communion and she'd tell him her legs were just too bad for her to get to church and climb all those stairs at Holy Angels.

Her legs were not so bad, however, that she couldn't travel and she treated her retirement in 1960, when she was sixty-two, like a shot from a starter's pistol. Nana had taken time off to raise a family. But, fiercely independent, she went back to work after her children were grown. Even after I was born, she took jobs in such places as the Hot Shoppes cafeteria (serving succotash) and at the Great Eastern Mills bargain store (putting prices on Hot Wheels cars). But she developed wanderlust when the Social Security checks started coming. She and her friend Anna DeProspo,

a short, dark woman with a real humdinger of a
mustache—one that was more Tom Selleck than Frida
Kahlo—took trips to Florida and Hawaii, not to mention a grand tour of Italy that Joe Mendillo—our local
tour operator, a sort of low-rent Mario Perillo—put
together for St. Anthony's Church in Paterson, where
Grandma Carmela and my unabashedly zaftig cousins
Mary and Day-Day went. The pictures of the two An-
nas in housedresses, bending over to feed pigeons in
the Piazza San Marco, are stunning, let me tell you.

They were good companions for each other, but
Grandma would always say: "Anna, why don't you use
a little Zip on your upper lip and get rid of that mustache?" (Zip was Nana's depilatory of choice.) Her
friend would say in a grand, well-rehearsed manner,
"God put it there, *who am I to take it away?*" She
never budged . . . or Zipped . . . and took her mustache to her grave.

Whenever Anna and Nana returned from one of
their package-deal jaunts, Nana would assemble a
scrapbook. With Scotch tape, she would affix post-
cards, brochures, matchbooks, "Do Not Disturb"
signs, "Occupato" signs from the airplane, and whatever else she'd stuck into her white patent pocketbook
while she traveled. On one page you'd have pictures
of the Pope; on the next, a postcard of Sergio Franchi
and Corbett Monica. She would write "NANA'S
TRAVELS" on the front page, in pencil. She gave me
one of her scrapbooks one afternoon while she was

cleaning her closets. Instead of writing something sentimental as a dedication, she wrote: "Frankie, if you don't want this, throw it out. Love, Nana."

She had a big heart—especially for me—but she could be meaner than anyone if she didn't like you. Jostled on a crowded checkout line, she'd announce, "This Puerto Rican is pushing me!" loud enough for the entire store to hear. Once, uninvited to the wedding of one of our Southern Italian cousins, a particularly dark-skinned girl, she vowed never to speak to "that Negro" again. Even I got called "Little Sissy Frankie," when I decided G.I. Joe needed a makeover and tried sewing doll clothes on my mother's Singer. Nana was resplendent in her meanness, though. She used to watch *Wheel of Fortune,* and whenever someone unappealing to her spun the wheel, she'd shout "Bankrupt! Bankrupt! Bankrupt!" If they did, in fact, land on Bankrupt and lose all their money she would say "Yesssssss!" and slap the arm of her chair with devilish delight. If they won, she'd get pissed off, get up from her favorite rocker in the sunroom, and announce with a flourish: "I'm going down to the dungeon!"

She really was Grandpa Munster with a permanent wave.

From her not-quite-subterranean lair in our white-shingled version of 1313 Mockingbird Lane, she ruled the roost. Like her TV alter ego, Nana knew her son-in-law, the supposed head of our household, was really a softhearted pushover. Frank Senior—as big a goof-ball as Herman Munster himself, in her eyes—pretended to be an unfeeling, unsentimental tough, but he was no match for her strong will or my mother's equally forceful nature. I didn't figure that out until I'd left for college. But I got my first inkling when I was just past two. That was when I realized that our lives on Prospect Street were not impervious to tragedy and that, unfortunately, things didn't work themselves out in the thirty minutes allotted them on television. The week that the Munsters pondered relocating the family to Buffalo—in an episode called "Munsters on the Move"—my father decided to relocate, too. That week, much to our horror, he moved into a semi-private room at a hospital in Paterson.

On
Corduroy,
Walking
Backwards

*I*t was the morning
of March 23, 1965, when Frank Senior went to see
Dr. Selikoff and, while sitting on the paper-lined ex-
amining table having an electrocardiogram, decided to
have a heart attack. Right then and there. At forty-
two years old. Politely, quietly, and conveniently.

You have to applaud his timing.

Realizing what was happening, they rushed him to
Barnert Memorial Hospital in Paterson, where Dr.
Joelson, the cardiologist, kept him for three weeks of
observation. For twenty-one days, my mother traipsed
back and forth during visiting hours, while I clung to
Nana, my four-foot-tall pillar of fortitude, at home.
Even with her to keep me busy, those days without
my father seemed endless and unsure. Without his

gorilla-hairy arms to hold me, our house seemed for the first time vulnerable. Things weren't as they should have been. *That*, I could sense. The first night my father didn't come home, I crept into my parents' bed, to calm my fears as much as those of the henna-haired forty-five-year-old I was curled up next to. Marian, like me, was terrified that our big, strong man was never coming back.

The Frank Senior who *did* return from Barnert was not the same man who left. After his heart attack, my father didn't pursue any of the things he enjoyed. He wasn't the three-pack-a-day Winstons smoker he had been—he stopped paying thirty-two cents a pack, cold turkey—and he began laying off his favorite drink, Dewar's White Label. He'd faced his own mortality and been told by his doctor that he'd never be as good as new; the sparkle went out of his chocolate-brown eyes with their long, long caterpillar lashes. He had made it through World War II unscathed—seen concentration camps; fought Nazis—but facing death at a time when he'd just begun to raise a family was too much for him.

My father's heart attack confirmed what Nana had surmised all along: For all his huff-and-puff bravado, all his Italian machismo, Frank Senior was just a nervous-stomached softie. He would never be life-by-the-balls bold, like her, or a glutton for new experiences, like me. But he was always good-hearted, even when his heart was broken. Marian called him St. Francis of Assisi.

Frank Senior was frail when he returned; his face, with its overzealous nose and forehead that stopped behind his ears, was paler; the thick mat of hair on his chest now covered a thinner frame atop the skinny bowed legs he always said a pig could run through. My father was clearly shaken up by the turn of events his relatively young life had taken. His mother had died while still in her forties. He worried a similar fate would befall him.

While my father was in the hospital, Marian busied herself, finding strength in redecorating. She'd ordered some new wall-to-wall carpeting to surprise my father, which it did. But it was nothing like the surprise I gave him two months later. I was feeling slighted by all the attention my father was receiving during his first weeks back home, so I decided to do something that would bring all eyes back to me. So in May, on a sunny Saturday morning, when I was two and a half, I tried to kill myself.

Well, sort of.

My father and I had decided to go to Valley Spa, where he bought the newspaper every morning and shot the bull with Bud, the white-aproned galoot who owned the place, and Johnny R., the shortened-named short order cook who was a cousin of ours and could fry cheeseburgers with the best of them. Our car, a

33

blue 1964 Chevy Impala, was parked at the top of our steep hill of a driveway with the engine running and me in my car seat, ready to go. But Frank had forgotten something inside the house and ran back, leaving me alone. He figured I'd be all right.

What could go wrong in sixty seconds? A lot, as it turns out.

Curious about what would happen, I began to look longingly at the gearshift. With all my might, I pulled the lever down and put the car into reverse. It began to roll backwards down the hill, slowly picking up speed. At this point, I realized that my plea for attention had backfired, and that I was going to die. Terrified, I started to wail.

Hearing my cries, Frank Senior came running out, saw what was happening, and tried to jump into the car. Instead, he slipped, and couldn't reach the brake pedal no matter how hard he tried. With one hand on the steering wheel and the other hanging on to the door, he tried to drag his foot and stop the car like some man of steel. But that didn't work. We continued to roll toward Prospect Street. At the last second, my father guided the car into a giant forsythia bush in our neighbors Ann and John Hanley's front yard across the street. With only minor damage to the plant and the skid marks of one scuffed shoe drawn in a line down the driveway, my tarnished but healing hero had saved me.

Frank Senior grabbed me, went inside, and gulped down a shot of Scotch, which was always kept under the kitchen sink next to a half-full bottle of pink Vel and a can of Comet, just for emergencies like this one. He'd sworn off the stuff only a few months earlier, but this was a much-deserved reward. We sat at the kitchen table, relieved and reunited, happy to be a family, more or less unharmed. It was a close call with a happy ending.

In those days of my childhood, and in the years that immediately followed, it was easy to love my father, a big lug who hated only two things in the whole world: dogs sniffing his crotch, and stepping in chewing gum. He despised dogs, but they gravitated to him as if he were St. Francis of Assisi. They'd nuzzle his nuts and Frank Senior would say "Get the hell outta here," running all the words together and stressing the first syllable. Whenever a wayward piece of Juicy Fruit ended up under his Florsheims, which always seemed to happen when we went shopping together, he'd say, "Sonofabitch," and then make a big overblown production out of scraping it off. It was as if gum on your sole were the worst thing in the world.

Every night, my father would yawn, without fail saying "Oh gee whiz" as he exhaled—a hint of the boyishness he once harbored—and decide it was time for bed. Clumsily, he'd kiss me, sandpaper for a face. "G'night, buddy," he'd say, and trail off to the bed-

room, skinny legs sticking out from shorty pajamas. He had the most beautiful, soft, porcelain-white feet —the only part of him, other than his head, that wasn't covered with hair.

I felt safe standing on those feet, lifted up by my father's hairy arms. My toes bare on his corduroy slippers, I'd walk backwards, one giant step, then another. I was a miniature carbon copy of the man, weightless against his hairy legs as he traipsed down the hall to his room. We might as well have been on the moon, doing our little backwards dance to dreamland, I felt so high, but tethered to him. He smelled of baby powder and cotton pajamas washed in Tide, clean but like a man. I was too young then to recognize the differences between us, or imagine the rifts and arguments we would have. We were still like one then, a father and son impressed with each other. Family life —still new for a couple who had been childless for so long—was something wondrous to share.

During my father's twelve weeks at home, recuperating from his heart attack, Marian ran our house like a sick ward, forcing me to be quiet and forbidding Frank Senior any sort of physical exertion. He couldn't putter around the house or work under the hood of his car. And sex was clearly out of the question. My mother set him up in the guest room, which we called the spare room. He agreed to this because he didn't want to disturb my mother when he got up at night. The truth, as I later found out, was that after his heart attack she was afraid to sleep with him, and he knew it. It scared Marian to lie there listening to her husband breathe and worrying that he suddenly might stop.

My parents made excuses to themselves and to me about not catching each other's colds thanks to their separate bedrooms. I believed them. But years later I realized the separation was symptomatic of a growing distance between my father and the rest of the family. It was the beginning of a pattern in which mother and son became best friends to make up for the withdrawn attention we so needed from Frank Senior but could never get.

We never called the spare room my father's room, even though he always slept there. To do so would have been to acknowledge the permanence of that arrangement—Mother in the master bedroom, Father in the guest room—but that's the way it would always be. And from then on, I took turns sleeping with my mother for a few nights, then my father for a few, me always restless and slugging it out in my sleep. Each morning, I'd hear a report of just how much trouble I'd been. "You punched me right in the back," my mother would say. They tried to get me to sleep in my own bed, but I was too afraid to be left alone. They would try petting me like a puppy until I fell asleep, but as soon as they stopped, I'd wake up and start crying. They'd relent and I'd be in one of their beds for another night. I slept with one or the other

almost every night until I hit puberty, but never told anyone.

It was my secret—and theirs—for years.

In July 1965, when Frank returned to work after his heart attack, the company switched him from production control to the shipping department and cut his pay from $149 to $124 a week, telling him he couldn't work as hard now that he had a heart condition, so they didn't have to pay him as much. This was a lot of malarkey, as he would say, but there was no union to back him up, so there was little he could do about it. He didn't have the fight left in him. Frank Senior stopped wearing white shirts to work; his ties were saved for Sunday mornings.

But every day Pop would get up and drive a mile to the plant, smelling of Old Spice and Ivory soap, getting there by seven-thirty, coming home for lunch and *Jeopardy* at noon, and returning between four and four-thirty P.M., his car rounding the corner of First Avenue, a copy of the *Daily News* on the front seat with the Jumble puzzle filled in. He was an expediter, a glorified name for the kind of mail-room clerk so many professionals only notice when they need them to do something. He always felt like he'd gotten the shaft. That cut in pay was a blow as much to his masculinity as to his wallet.

With my father gone most of the day, I was surrounded by women—Marian, Nana, and, on some days, Aunt Angie—who kept me too busy to pine for Frank Senior's return from work. As I grew, I became closer to them than to my father, and I do believe Marian liked it that way. When she was a kid, her father used to give away her toys whenever company came over. If they had a child and came to visit, they left with one of Marian's things, no matter how beloved it was. But now that she was a parent, no one, not even my father, was going to take her favorite plaything—me—away from her.

My mother always let my father know that she loved him, but she made it quite clear that she loved *me* more. Marian never acknowledged that love for a husband was different from love for a son; she just doled it out in unequal portions. What I wanted as much as her love, though, was a share of my father's attention. But once I stopped being a toddler, I could never get it. After a day's work, Frank Senior only cared about watching sports on TV and playing the ponies. My interests in the arts and culture and cooking—things my father called "womanly"—never rubbed off on him. He didn't even like the TV shows I liked, dismissing them by saying "Who the hell wants to watch that?" Marian and Nana and I would watch things together. My father would fall asleep on the couch and snore instead, mouth gaping, his body wrapped in an acrylic granny square afghan blanket, while Merv Griffin and Arthur Treacher kibitzed.

When he had his heart attack, Frank Senior

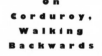

stopped dreaming and lost any semblance of playful-
ness he ever had. It was as if he'd seen the ceiling and
it was closing in on him. The stars were too far out
of reach for him to even be bothered with them anymore. He closed off the outside world, choosing instead to remain where it was safe and manageable.
Turning cynical as he grew older—and faced with a
fanciful son whose grip on reality was loosened by fairy
stories and Saturday-morning television—my father
would ask me "When is your bubble gonna burst?"
And, when I would tell him I was wishing for
something—a new toy or, later, a life away from Little
Falls—he'd say "Wish in one hand and shit in the
other and see which one fills up first!" It was his way
of saying that if I didn't expect much from life I
wouldn't be disappointed, like he was.

Although my father could be very funny and gen-
erous in everything but his affections, he became a
killjoy over the years, taking the pleasure out of things
for everyone if he couldn't enjoy them himself.
Whether it was food or a Disneyland fantasy, he pissed
all over it. We were on vacation one year at one of
those historical villages where you don't learn anything, but you *do* get to buy candles and potpourri.
Marian and I had wandered off together and gone into
an old-fashioned ice cream parlor. We ordered hot
fudge sundaes, with coffee ice cream for her and banana for me. Just as they arrived, stunning us with the

height of their whipped-creamed splendor, my father poked his head in the door. Before we could even savor our first cold-sweet bite, his voice boomed across the restaurant: "You *really* need that!" He made us feel like a couple of fatsos, but we ate the sundaes anyway. Not with glee; we ate them out of spite.

Frank Senior didn't like being the third wheel. But, if he felt excluded, he brought it on himself. He was unwilling to bridge the gap between his experience and mine. I always imagined that if my father and I had gone to high school together, instead of forty years apart, he would have beaten me up. If not that, he surely wouldn't have done anything to stop those who did. As boys, we were that different.

He grew up a real guy-guy—a hairy, nicotine-fueled, baseball-playing, linseed-oil-smelling, bowling-enthusiastic man. He hated to read and write. He lived life unquestioningly, and believed, as I never could, that enough *was* enough. All I ever wanted was more, and that irked him. Whenever we went to Pinebrook Amusement Park, my father would say, "If I took you on six rides, you'd want to go on seven." And it was true. I wanted everything, and everything was more than he could give me.

It is clear that we were not meant for each other, Frank Senior and me. He was practical—a realist. I was fanciful—a dreamer. He grew up wanting to be Babe Ruth. I dreamed of being Batgirl because she had a fringe-trimmed motorcycle *and* a red flip wig. He expected to have a son who was a little tough guy, or at least a kid who could catch. I wanted a father who'd be my date for *Dreamgirls*, someone who liked browsing through designer sportswear at Bloomingdale's. But what can you do? Like most homosexual sons and heterosexual fathers, we were stuck with each other.

I can only imagine what he must have thought when, as a child, I put on my mother's fake fur—a minky little three-quarter-length swing number with big buttons—and her white gloves, grabbed Binky and Squeezy, my stuffed bunnies, sat them on the couch, and pretended we were going shopping. Or when I would take all the pots and pans out of the cupboard, scatter them across the kitchen floor as if it were one big linoleum cooktop, and pretend to be getting ready for a lavish dinner party.

Still, I did try, at times, to be my father's son. One year I joined Little League. I was on a team sponsored by Great Notch Fuel. For the first time, I could feel my father's pride. But quite predictably, I was a terrible ballplayer, no matter how hard I tried. His offers to practice with me after school would almost always end up with me crying because I'd been hit in the head by a missed fly ball. As the season progressed, my crying became a regular occurrence. At least once each game I'd end up crying my eyes out, feeling like a failure. I was so bad that they created a position for me—roving outfielder. I was so far away from the action, I couldn't do any damage: I was stationed in the parking lot. No one ever hit balls out that far.

Miraculously, I made it through an entire season. But in the car on the way home from the ball field following the final game of the season, I confessed to my father, as if he didn't already know, just how much I hated playing baseball. I had let him down. But I couldn't face another season, even if he thought I was as big a klutz as the kids did.

"Why did you sign up in the first place?" he asked me, turning his head toward me, then quickly back, taking his eyes off the road for only a second, hairy hands gripping the steering wheel.

"For you," I told him, fighting back tears and looking straight ahead.

"Don't ever do *anything* just for me," he said.

My father could not have said anything sweeter or more understanding than that. With an orange-red sun fading beyond the Quik-Chek on Main Street and then the Gulf station at the bottom of First Avenue, his words surprised me. As he turned the corner towards home, Frank Senior knew that Frank Junior would never follow in his footsteps, any more than I would ever again walk backwards on his corduroy slippers. He hadn't planned on a heart attack or on a son who couldn't play baseball, but he'd have to make do.

I was relieved and only too happy to have my after-

school afternoons free again. It meant that instead of baseball practice, I could spend more time with the precocious little girl named Heidi, who was my first best friend. From the day I met her in Mrs. Banks's A.M. kindergarten class, I liked her better than anyone I'd ever met in Little Falls.

**L o i s ,
D o n ,
a n d
H e i d i**

*H*eidi was my first lesbian, although neither of us knew that in 1967 when we met over blocks and then sat next to each other in kindergarten. She was the cutest little girl— a freckle-faced roughhouser with brown curly hair who wore sky-blue vinyl dresses and packed a punch like nobody's business. I loved her as much as I loved Binky and Squeezy, my go-cart fire engine, and my bottle-green fake snakeskin vest combined, which was a lot.

On the playground, near the swings, the Teutonic little tomboy would say, "Let's see who can hit the lightest," and then, with all her might, she'd sock whoever was dumb enough to fall for it. Usually that was me. Then she'd laugh a husky laugh and say, "I lose!" as if it were the funniest thing in the whole world. It wasn't, and the black-and-blue marks on my arms proved it. I bit her once to get even. She cried, but my vengeful chomping was as much an act of love as her punches had been. I was smitten with Heidi from the get-go. She was all I could ever want in a boy and all I ever *would* want in a girl.

She was smart, funny as all get-out, and I now realize, as butch as I was femme. She didn't fit into our surroundings any better than I did. In the first grade, when I went to the hospital to have my tonsils out, she sent me a note, written on that gray-beige paper with lines at the bottom and space at the top for a picture. It said, "I like you and you like me. I will buy you a toy." At six, that was my idea of love.

We were fated to be together. Everyone from my grandmother to the lady who rented us shoes at the bowling alley said so, predicting that we'd become childhood sweethearts and then get married one day and live in Little Falls like everyone else did. We *were* soul mates, born eleven days apart, both under the sign of Scorpio. Before we knew each other, we'd gone to the same pediatrician, Dr. Cardulo, whose office was miles away in Packanack Lake. When I discovered this coincidence, and because Heidi's parents were considerably younger than mine, I liked to pretend we'd been switched during our first routine checkup and were sent home with the wrong parents. I desperately wanted to be a part of their family, mostly because of

Heidi's mother, Lois, and the magic she was able to weave into the synthetic-blend fabric of our lives.

They lived only a few houses away from School #1, in a two-story white house with a porch painted battleship gray. It wasn't as fancy as our house—no gold sconces or animal-carved armchairs—but there was wonder in that house, thanks to Lois, who wrote and illustrated children's books and, best of all, moved through the world like a character in one of them. In her eyes, pineapple ducks sported peppermint bills, trees wore bubble gum leaves, doggy dentists performed hound's-tooth checks, and magic lima beans needed only a rub to unleash their powers. When the reception was bad on her TV, she'd say: "It's coming in in tweed."

Lois was eccentric and looked it. In a practice that was controversial for Little Falls, she wore a different wig every day, and no two were alike. She might sport a brunette *That Girl* flip on Tuesday, and a blond Carol Brady shag on Friday. You never knew what you were going to get when you rang their doorbell. She'd answer in some sort of hair creation and full makeup, with false eyelashes like butterflies. These she applied before a True-to-Light mirror, the kind with three different adjustable light levels—office, daylight, and dusk. With this mirror, as enchanting as the Magic Mirror that Miss Louise used to see her TV audience on *Romper Room*—Lois made sure she looked perfect for all her activities. When she wasn't writing or painting, she volunteered at a mental hospital and trained as a eucharistic minister at church. Their house, never a window open, was frosty cool all summer, toasty in winter. It was a good place to be creative. The outside world didn't interfere there. Not in the beginning, anyway.

Heidi's father, Don, was an engineer, although what that meant I didn't really know, except that he had invented some sort of circuit-board thing and made a lot more money than my father ever would. He was a bit of a nerd, really, someone who said, "There's an idear," whenever he had one. But inside his Wally Cox body beat the heart of an adventurer. For one thing, he rode a motorcycle and, once in a while, would take me out for a spin. It was thrilling. He and Lois lived with six cats and two grandparents, who, in their apartment upstairs, seemed oblivious to the colorful antics of the cast of characters one floor below them. They probably had no idea they were living above a female drag queen, a chopper-riding Milquetoast, a future lesbian, and her always-there friend, who was a pansy just waiting to flower.

Needless to say, my parents were always wary of this group. But when I was six, Heidi's family was everything I wanted mine to be—comfortable in its queerness and unabashedly modern. This was a generational thing, although at the time, I didn't realize it. Unlike my parents, who were really part of Heidi's grandparents' era, Lois and Don were hungry for the future and unafraid of change. In their house on Stevens Avenue, there was a sense of flux, while at our place on Prospect, our cordoned-off-living-room life reeked of stagnation. Our house looked forever the same—Italian provincial. But Heidi's was always changing. You'd go away for a few days and come back to find her bedroom completely redone. There'd be peel-and-stick white plastic bricks where perched-eagle early American wallpaper had been only days before. And, although she, too, was an only child, there might be bunk beds where a pullout couch had been. New was good in the world of Lois, Don, and Heidi. My family, on the other hand, believed in holding on to whatever you had for dear life and never letting go. Progress frightened my parents . . . but not me.

While my father read *American Legion* magazine, each issue with a Haband ad for guayabera shirts on the back cover, Don read *Playboy*. My mother read *Better Homes & Gardens* and clipped recipes for Harvey Wallbanger cake. Lois read *Cosmopolitan* and took sex quizzes and read how-to advice on keeping relationships hot. I'll never forget when Lois brought home the first issue of *Playgirl* in 1974. I was mesmerized by my first glimpse of adult male flesh and, much to Heidi's consternation, tried my darnedest to spend as much time looking through it and subsequent issues as I could. When her mother's Volkswagen bug would venture up the gravel driveway or her grand-

Lois,
Don,
and
Heidi

49

mother would make her way slowly down the stairs, I'd put the *Playgirls* away, but not a minute before. I was hooked, a voyeur at twelve. I hadn't been that excited since Heidi bought Carly Simon's *No Secrets* album, with that picture of the singer with hard nipples on the cover.

Even without the magazines, there was an air of sexual activity in that house. It was steamy compared to ours. Don and Lois took "naps" together in the afternoon. Not that we heard any huffing and puffing: they were very discreet. But Heidi and I knew something more than napping was up. There was romance. Lois and Don went to the movies as if they were still dating. They seemed like lovers, not just pals like my parents. Once they invited Marian and Frank to join them at the movies. My parents insisted the children come along, so Heidi and I insisted on picking the movie. All six of us went to see *The Poseidon Adventure*, in which Shelley Winters turns upside down and then drops dead. It was scary, but Heidi and I loved being out with the grown-ups, three couples all in a row, a bucket of popcorn in my lap, a Tab in Heidi's, hiding our eyes during the gruesome parts and waiting for Maureen McGovern to sing "The Morning After."

At breakfast the morning after our triple date, Marian and Frank seemed uncomfortable with the night before. I had so wanted them to enjoy it, but a movie and dinner was not their scene, even if it was Lois and Don and Heidi and Frankie's. The one other time my parents and I went to the movies together, we saw *The Gang That Couldn't Shoot Straight.* The picture's big laugh involved a four-foot-tall Italian woman with a butcher knife chasing a man who'd slept with her daughter. "Put it on the table, I'll cut it off!" she screamed. For anyone else, this was a Mafia comedy. For my father, it was a movie about my grandmother, a little too close for comfort.

With Lois, Don, and Heidi—and without my parents—I would eat many a dinner at the Wedgwood Cafeteria in Montclair, which wasn't far away but was a heck of lot more cosmopolitan than anything in Little Falls, the ziti-and-meatballs capital of northern New Jersey. Actually, the place was just less Italian than eating at home, which, to me, meant it was better. It was upscale as cafeterias go, with real napkins and the kind of overcooked peas and carrots that no one has ever managed to improve upon. Although my parents disapproved of their lavishness, Heidi's parents would pay for everything, even for the butter pats that cost an extra three cents apiece and the chocolate pudding parfaits. When it was just the three of us—Lois, Heidi, and me—we'd go to Bonds for tuna melts and Awful Awfuls, ice cream shakes that the menu described as "Awful Big and Awful Good."

Before it was common to do so, Heidi and her family ate out almost every night. They had no choice. Lois was one of the worst cooks ever to pick up a wooden spoon. Her two signature recipes were Sheila's

tuna fish salad, which was a can of tuna and half a
container of plain yogurt whirred in a blender until
you could practically drink it, and microwave chocolate cake made with a Duncan Hines mix. This always
came out looking like the dark side of the moon, an
inch thick on one end, three inches thick on the other.
Lois would even things out with ready-to-spread frosting and sprinkles and we would eat it like it was the
best cake in the world. My mother's cakes were perfect
but boring. Heidi's mother's cakes were an adventure,
a culinary disaster dished up like a horror movie on a
plate. The best was one she called the *Exorcist* cake.
The frosting was a barfy pea green.

Lois encouraged such ingenuity, taking a cake that
flopped and turning it into something wondrous. She
believed in creativity and imagination, smiling on all
sorts of eccentric behavior my parents thought only to
stifle. Lois was an earth mother with her head in the
clouds, someone who made my mother and father
seem hopelessly Old World, too traditional for my
good. I thought they would die when Lois brought
home matching Ultrasuede fringed vests for Heidi and
me, hers with a Minnie Mouse appliqué on the chest,
mine with a Mickey. Hippie fringe wasn't their style,
but for a while it was ours.

Heidi and I did everything together over the years:
getting in trouble for calling Mrs. Paddock, our sixth-
grade teacher, Mrs. Little Green Sprout; doing
ceramics in Heidi's basement and getting light-headed

from the paint fumes; battling kids who picked on us because we were smart or weird or both. Our intelligence and our eccentricity made us targets in the neighborhood. And that only brought us closer. Even when it came to romance, Heidi and I ventured forth together. She knew stuff—particularly about sex—before any of the other kids. And she developed fast, too. By fifteen, Heidi was the bearer of the most amazing upper frontals in Little Falls, and she could kiss better than anyone. I know because she gave me lessons. We kissed a lot, first on my mother's purple couch, then sprawled on my bed with the lights off until my father came to make sure things weren't getting too out of hand. If he had known his son was going to be gay, and his son's first girlfriend was going to be a lesbian, he might have let us go all the way, hoping we'd hit it off sexually and spare him the heartache. But he didn't know, and neither did we, actually, nebulous in our sexuality then. It was very fun, but it was not to be. So much would not turn out the way we thought it would.

Heidi's mother would develop breast cancer, and thanks to chemotherapy her wigs became a necessity, not an expression of her many delicious moods. While Lois battled the disease that would prove fatal, Don met and fell in love with another woman and left the seemingly happy family of which, for so many years, I'd wanted to be a part. Heidi was devastated, feeling not like the doted-on only child she had been, but like an orphan. Compared to that, Marian and Frank's immutability seemed to me like safety, their white-knuckle clutch on tradition like stability. After all the wishing away I'd done, I realized I'd been born into the right family in the first place. By then, Heidi would gladly have traded the shards of her family life for the everyday wackiness of mine on Prospect Street.

Window
Dressing,
Cross-dressing,
and Christmas

*Y*ou could always tell
what holiday it was by the cardboard cutouts Scotch-
taped to the storm-door window facing out toward
Prospect Street. There were shamrocks and lepre-
chauns for St. Patrick's Day, a hopping brown bunny
for Easter, a majestic turkey—still alive and
feathered—and Pilgrims for Thanksgiving, a bust of a
bewigged George Washington for his birthday, and
one of Abraham Lincoln for his. We didn't miss any.

But the best decorations, hands down, were for
Halloween. Marian kept them in the attic in a large,
flat, almost coffinlike box of corrugated cardboard
printed to look like wood grain. Whenever I opened
it, a musty smell wafted out, as scary and sinister and
steeped in history as the stuff inside. There was a four-
foot-tall jointed witch in striped Mary Quant leggings,

a jack-o'-lantern in paisley bell-bottoms and buckled shoes, black cats with their backs arched, and an almost life-sized cardboard skeleton with arms and legs you could pose any way you liked. We had skull-shaped candles, too, and hollow plastic pumpkins, crepe-paper ribbons in orange and black, and a black-light poster of the Frankenstein monster who looked like, but wasn't, "Frightenin' Frankie" from the *Groovie Goolies* cartoon I loved to watch on Saturday mornings. This show was about Sabrina, the teenaged witch who was a friend of the Archies. Betty and Veronica didn't know her secret. At the time, no one knew mine either.

Each year, we'd begin planning our costumes at about the same time Herb, who ran the paper store near School #1, got in his yearly supply of wax lips and orange paraffin whistles in late September. You'd hear them on the playground during recess—one of the older kids would always be first to have one—and know you had to get yours that day, too. Heidi and I, although best friends, were always in competition with each other to see who could come up with the best costume. But I would always win a prize at the St. Agnes's Church Halloween party and she wouldn't.

The problem was that Lois made costumes that were *too* good. They were so creative, so out-of-the-ordinary that no one knew quite what they were. "*Che cazzo è questo?* Is she supposed to be a vampire or a scarecrow?" my grandmother would wonder. Heidi was supposed to be a "vampire-scarecrow," Lois would say, but few in Little Falls were open to such an original hybrid. Although it was very cool, no one got it.

My costumes were more traditional. My first, when I was two, was that of a jungle cat with little kitty ears sticking out of the top of my hood. It was head-to-toe leopard print, which, if you're going to grow up to be gay, is not a bad way to start cross-dressing. We borrowed the costume from Aunt Angie, naturally. For my first big Halloween photo op, they posed me next to a big plastic pumpkin, its gap-toothed grin as wide as my own.

It was a long time before they let me be that fey again.

Instead, over the years, I made my way through all the macho costumes there were. Every boy did. I was a hobo—face all dirty, clothes clean but patched; then a cowboy; then an Indian with war-painted stripes on my face that you needed cold cream to wash off. I wore a store-bought Ben Cooper–brand skeleton costume with a plastic mask and a white jumpsuit with black flocked bones on the front to Mrs. Banks's kindergarten class. The following year, Marian took a plastic lion mask, sewed one of my father's socks to the back, and then tufted the sock with brown yarn so I had a major mane. I wore gold pajamas with a tail attached, a matching brown tuft of yarn at the end. I won a prize in the Halloween parade, which always started on the school playground and ended in the park near our house. All the kids went.

My favorite costume ever was Dracula, because everyone (except my father) pitched in to put it together. It was 1969 and I used my Thingmaker set—the make–your–own–Creepy Crawlers toy that all kids seriously burned themselves on that year—to make rubber bats and spiders to sew on my outfit, and long nails, and a third eye for my forehead. (My version of Dracula had glamour-length nails and especially good vision for some reason.) Nana cut an old black floor-length skirt up one side and made a cape, lining it with pale green satin and sewing a frog closure at the neck to attach it. Mom did my makeup, making my skin ghostly white, slicking my hair back, and painting in a black widow's peak just like Eddie Munster's, and giving my little-boy lips a blood-red going-over. I wore black pants and a turtleneck. Needless to say, I won a prize for that costume, too. Heidi, the vampire-scarecrow, was not pleased. "Lois, how could he win? He doesn't even go to this church, we do! It's not fair!" she complained.

The next year, I did drag for the first time. I wanted to be a witch, not a warlock, a *girl* witch, like Witchiepoo on *H. R. Pufnstuf*, which was my favorite show that year. Frank Senior wasn't exactly pleased with my desire to cross gender lines, but Marian saw no harm. It wasn't like I put on dresses in the middle of July.

(That came later, and I only did it once. It was an orange floor-length halter. I couldn't help myself.) Anyway, that Halloween, I wore a black crepe dress of my mother's, a long gray wig made of polyester fiberfill that we got in the seasonal department at Tops, my Dracula cape from the year before, and a pointed cardboard hat with a black cat against an October moon on the front. It had been an orange hat, but at my urging, Marian painted it black, except for the moon. It was way better black. My father even helped that year, spray-painting an old broom black for me to carry.

I was a big hit as a girl. So the next year I cross-dressed again. I donned my mother's same black dress and had Marian wrap the gray wig into a bun. I was Maudie Frickert, the Jonathan Winters granny character from TV. Heidi wouldn't tell me what her costume was, except that it was going to be good. When I picked her up to go to the Halloween parade, she was dressed as the marvelous, magical Burger King. One had just opened in Little Falls. She had a golden crown, red hair, and a regal robe and was carrying a Whopper the size of a hubcap that Lois had made from Styrofoam and tissue paper. It was her year to win, and she did. I was jealous, but her costume *was* better than mine. We posed for pictures—a victorious Heidi with her giant hamburger, and me with my purse: a future lesbian in pop-culture drag and a homo-to-be in a granny dress with a doily for a collar.

Every year on Halloween night, we would go out
in groups of three or four without our parents. We'd
heard stories of razor blades in apples and kids getting
poisoned Pixie Straws candy, but we didn't really
worry and neither did they. Heidi's parents did,
though, and insisted on chaperoning her, which really
wasn't cool. I went with the boys instead, sometimes
dodging eggs from some of the older kids who hadn't
wreaked enough havoc the night before, on what we
called Goosie Night. We'd make the rounds, the
crunching of leaves punctuated by singsong shouts of
"Trick or Treat!," trudging up Second Avenue to Dr.
Ferguson's house and Mrs. Presby's, down First as far
as Mr. Wren's, over to Lincoln, where Mrs. Hill would
always invite us in for a doughnut and cider. Then,
on the way back, we'd hit the Hanleys and the Ivanses,
then pass my house and go to the Capomaggis', to
Mrs. Brown's (she was the substitute teacher), and
then, always-always-always, to Rose Tosone's house
last. Rose was my mother's best girlfriend, an extrav-
agant woman who not only gave out full-sized candy
bars long after everyone else had switched to "fun
size," but would stick a dollar or two in my bag when
she saw it was me. Nothing was a better finale to an
evening of trick-or-treating than a visit to her carpeted
foyer. You knew you'd get something good. As if that
weren't enough, Marian would be waiting at home
with some kind of surprise—maybe a devil's food layer
cake with fudge icing decorated with candy corn, all

orange, white, and brown, alternating in a perfect border around the top. We'd have tea and sort through my goody bag. Nana would usually join us—in costume. One year, she came up from the dungeon dressed as a pregnant bride, with a pillow shoved under a satin dress.

"How much did Rose give you?" Nana would ask.

"Two bucks and a three-pack of Reese's Peanut Butter Cups."

"Well, she's got it to give away," Nana would say, and then slip me a fin so as not to be outdone by anyone.

Almost the very next day, I would set my sights on Christmas, although in between there was my birthday (another layer cake and more goodies a week after Halloween) and Thanksgiving, when Papa Vic and his whole family would come for dinner. But Christmas was it. I couldn't wait for those decorations to come out. It was the most art-directed holiday there was. No strands of cranberries and popcorn for us; we bought big, fat silver tinsel garland at the Fountains of Wayne Christmas emporium, and hung it like Las Vegas. More was always better at Christmas. Even my father got into it. Frank Senior might have been a spoilsport eleven months of the year, but in December he played right along with us, enjoying himself even if it killed him to do so.

He was in charge of the Christmas tree. A week or

Window
Dressing,
Cross-
dressing,
and
Christmas

61

two before the holiday, he would get it out of the attic and put it together. Our tree was a seven-foot-tall broomstick covered with holes to poke evergreen-colored bottle-washer branches into. Branches were color-coded and so were the holes, so you always got a perfect conical shape. You really couldn't screw it up—except that one year when the paint wore off and the tree came out so crooked that it looked like we were celebrating a German Expressionist Christmas. But that was much later.

Anyway, when the tree was together, we'd wrap it in lights—multicolored ones one year; all white, the next. Nana would invariably say, "It looks pretty just the way it is, don't put anything else on it." But we always would. First, the Liberace-approved garland was draped from branch to branch, then the blown-glass ornaments went on—some grapefruit-sized balls from the fifties, some shaped like Huckleberry Hound—until there wasn't a place that didn't glitter on any side of the tree. The tree stand rotated, so we *had* to decorate it all over. The year we got a silver aluminum tree and hung it with pink balls, we had a color-wheel spotlight to go with it.

That went around, too.

Underneath our slowly twirling glitzfest, we'd always create a snow scene, a mini North Pole with the queeniest elves and little cast-iron skaters on a mirror for a pond. Off to one side, we'd set up a Nativity scene. Grandpa Carney had built the manger we used, and it was all we had to remember him by. That, and my grandmother saying "He was no good, the *whoor-master.*"

Christmas Eve dinner was the big event, so important that we served it in our dining room, which we used six times a year, tops. A few days before the holiday, Nana would start soaking the *baccalà*, dried salt cod, in a big tub in the laundry room, changing the water during commercials of *The 4:30 Movie.* On Christmas Eve, she would batter-fry some of the flaky fish and make the rest into a salad with roasted peppers. She'd make five other kinds of fish, too, because you had to have seven different fish dishes on Christmas Eve. That was the tradition. That, and linguine with Progresso clam sauce and a visit from our non-Italian neighbors for Italian round cookies, fruit-cocktail cake, and coffee.

After our company left, we always put out cookies and milk for Santa, like you're supposed to. We would leave store-bought jelly-filled ones that I liked better than my mother's homemade ones. After I went to bed, unbeknownst to me, my mother would eat them. She always left a few crumbs on the plate so I would think Santa actually got to them. A nice touch. She'd drink the milk, too, even though she hated it, because she didn't want to waste it or take the chance that I'd notice it had been poured back into the container. She was right. I would have noticed. One year Santa actually visited during the day. This was completely out

Window
Dressing,
Cross-
dressing,
and
Christmas

63

of step with all I knew about him, but I didn't complain. It was my father in a plastic Santa mask and a suit he'd borrowed from a guy at work. But I was so shy about my first brush with celebrity that I didn't notice Santa's hands were as hairy as Dad's.

I was gullible like that, wanting to believe in magic for as long as I could. By the time I was eight years old, though, my father had other ideas. He decided it was time that I knew the truth about Santa Claus. So, on Christmas morning, although my mother begged him not to tell me, he spilled the beans.

"Frankie, you're old enough to know there is no Santa Claus," he said.

"No Santa? Where did all these presents come from, then?" I asked.

"Your mother bought them. She's the one who eats the cookies, too, like she really needs them with her figure."

In my blue-and-white-striped pajamas and Flintstone slippers, I was devastated, convinced Christmas would never be fun again. I was too young to understand that happiness didn't depend on whether anyone slid down our chimney or not. And my father was too unthinking to realize that if he'd told me on Arbor Day, I might not have been so upset on Christmas morning. I went crying to my mother, who held me and soothed me as best she could.

Then she let my father have it.

"*Everything* has to be grown-up with you," she said

to him, her face all hard and angry. "Didn't you ever have a childhood?"

Marian knew the answer to that. Frank Senior *hadn't* had much of one. His family was poor. His father was distant. His mother was too busy working to spend much time playing with him. Frank Senior wasn't going to rob me of my childhood, though. That Marian would make sure of, even if it meant excluding him. She set out to make up for that day, when he forced reality on me long before I was ready for such an intrusion. Only a couple of years later, Marian and I ventured off on our first vacation without Frank Senior. Instead, we went with both grandmothers and thirty-five other Italian-American senior citizens to Florida. What a trip that was.

Window
Dressing,
Cross-
dressing,
and
Christmas

Frankie Goes to Hollywood, Fla.

*O*ur lives changed when we got the Chrysler, the first new car my folks bought after I was born. It was a 1969 white four-door Newport, a big beautiful boat, with a black vinyl roof, a black vinyl interior, and an AM radio that had these cool silver dial-adjusters instead of knobs. It wasn't as sexy as the Mercury Cougar that my mother's friend Two-Face Dot—"the big phony"—drove, with its blink-blink-blink directionals, but it was pretty swift.

The Chrysler lacked only one feature: air-conditioning. There had been one "comfort-cooled" model on the lot the day my father bought it, but it was butter yellow—the same color as Booby and Peg Natale's Cadillac—and my mother didn't want to copy, especially considering that her *paisan* Booby's car was higher on the scale of Turtle Waxed luxury than ours.

Besides, she hated air-conditioning because for years she'd frozen her ass off every day at the beauty shop. "Air-conditioning is the reason I'm sick all the time," she said, even though she hadn't worked there in more than two years. We could just forget about having it in our new car. Marian had spoken.

The only *other* drawback of the Chrysler was that we had to use it.

We could not park it in the driveway and just admire it, proud owners that my parents were. No, we had to drive it, and not only to get from mass at Holy Angels to the Pine Brook Auction to buy a spit-roasted takeaway chicken for Sunday dinner. We had to drive it for my father's amusement. And so the Newport became a key player in all our recreational activities. Along with watching game shows every day while my father coached "Come on, you dumb bastard, bid higher!" and going to Grandpa's once a week to watch him hork into a Medaglia d'Oro coffee can next to his chair every few minutes—he had emphysema—we had to go for rides every Sunday.

My father loved to drive. Anywhere and nowhere.

This would have been fine if I hadn't been prone to motion sickness and if I hadn't had to sit in the backseat, which I always did because I was the kid. The rides would have been swell, too, if we'd actually had a destination in mind and stopped somewhere and did something when we got there. But no. Instead, we would drive for the sake of driving. And my father would whistle in that frigging vibrato of his over the sound of his favorite all-news radio station until I was green around the gills.

Sometimes he would admit that we were lost, and I'd have a panic attack, worried that we'd never find our way home. My father seemed to delight in watching me fret until he finally said he actually knew where we were and how we'd get back. Most times, though, our journeys were just routine loops through the by-ways of northern and central New Jersey. Perhaps we'd get as far as the Delaware Water Gap or Spring Valley, New York, where my father bought lottery tickets and cheap liquor at a place called Shopper's Paradise. That was a real thrill.

To alleviate the boredom of these trips, I would feign sleepiness and say I was going to take a nap and lie down and put a blanket over me. Instead of sleeping, I'd concentrate on the vibrations of the tires on the pavement, which made me as horny as a seven-year-old could be. Ever so quietly, with as little motion as I could, so Marian wouldn't turn around and notice and Frank wouldn't see anything in the rearview mirror, I'd touch myself. My face and body pressed into the crevice where the backseat and the seatback came together, I was a leatherette lover. It felt dirty and wicked and better than playing count the cows or license plates any day. My parents never realized what I was doing. They were just happy for the peace and quiet.

When we did have a destination in mind it was usually Great Gorge, a ski slope in New Jersey that, frankly, isn't that great or particularly gorgeous. We didn't ski or even entertain notions of going up to the lodge for a cup of Ovaltine. We didn't participate in any such thing. That would have been antithetical to my parents' way of life. They were watchers, not doers, quite comfortable on the sidelines—or in this case, at the bottom of a snow-covered slope. So we would stop the car and watch other people in brightly colored nylon pants and beefy sweaters ride the chairlift up and then schuss their way down. They seemed to be having so much fun, while we had our noses pressed to a car window as if we had not been invited. It was like TV, and that made my parents happy. Vicarious adventure. No real thrills, but no danger, either.

Marian would marvel at the bravery of even the littlest children on skis, but never thought that her own little kid might like to try it. We'd gawk for maybe half an hour, me kneeling on the backseat, with the car heater on up front. Then, having worked up an appetite watching other people exert themselves, we'd head to Paul's Diner in Parsippany. Eating was the sport at which the DeCaros excelled. I always ordered roast prime beef au jus from the giant menu. "Au jus," of course, I pronounced "awe-juss."

No one ever said "oh-zhoo" at Paul's.

I didn't mind our visits to Great Gorge so much once they opened a Playboy Club not far from there.

We'd go for special events like the annual recreational vehicles show, where Marian and Frank would ooh and aah over every Herculon-covered Hide-A-Bed. We traipsed in and out of Winnebagos and pop-up campers, enthralled by the adventurous lives they promised. But we couldn't afford to buy one, so we watched here, too. We did go into the actual Playboy Club one afternoon, when they opened it up to nonmembers. It seemed so dark and glamorous, all smoked glass and club chairs. The Bunnies were as scantily clad as the graffiti-covered dancers I liked so much on *Laugh-In*. I'd always fantasized about going to the *Laugh-In* cocktail party, where everyone danced and then froze like statues so someone could tell a joke. The Playboy Club was close enough. I was titillated beyond belief by all the exposed Bunny cleavage. When you're eight or ten years old, any hint of nudity does it for you.

The whole idea of sitting in a cocktail lounge, sipping Coke from a heavy highball glass with the Playboy logo on it, made me feel very classy, and my parents, too. My mother stole two shot glasses, three double old-fashioneds, and a half-dozen Bunny-head swizzle sticks that afternoon alone. Like every Italian-American woman I knew in those days, she carried a large handbag especially for such purposes. In our family, my mother was only a piker, though. In the petty-thievery department, Grandma Carmela was the pro. She could eat good for a week on one trip to an all-you-can-eat buffet, steal an ashtray to give as a present,

and grab enough sugar packets to bake a batch of pecan tassies besides.

Over the years, the Chrysler took us from one tourist attraction to another, especially places involving food. We made road trips to pretzel factories, candy plants, and breweries that turned out hundreds of cans of beer every hour. We also went to every sports hall of fame my father's cronies ever recommended. By the time I was thirteen, I'd learned more than I ever cared to about balls. Frank Senior hoped all this sports stuff would rub off on me, and I hoped it would, too. But, although I tried, I developed about as much enthusiasm for Joe DiMaggio's batting average as my father had for the career of Chita Rivera. There were always gift shops, though, and souvenirs made me happy no matter where they came from. The promise of shopping made even Cooperstown seem okay.

For our big trips, we headed south to Florida, which was always held up as some exotic land, spoken about in reverent tones by all our relatives. It wasn't as big a deal as California, where cousin June Marie lived, which they described in *mythical* terms. But as states go, Florida was someplace very special, somewhere where they had mermaid shows, and alligator farms, and, after a while, Walt Disney World.

It was worth the twenty-four-hour drive, car sickness and all.

On these trips to the Sunshine State, we would hit every hot spot from Saint Augustine to Hollywood to

Miami, and every tourist attraction from the Ponce de Leon Fountain of Youth to Cypress Gardens (with its water-skiing bathing beauties) and the Parrot Jungle, where you got to pose with four birds on your outstretched arms and one on your head. Parrots scared me to death, but my father made me do it anyway. Ever since, I've hated any bird you can't eat—Fred the cockatoo on *Baretta* included.

We went to Marineland my first time in Florida to see where they filmed *Flipper*. I loved that TV show, basically because I had a crush on the boy who played the older brother. The sight of him in wet denim cutoffs, his crotch pressed to his boogie board, was a high point of 1960s television for every gay boy in America. Whenever someone my age says he didn't know he was gay until he was in his twenties, I always say, "Didn't you watch *Flipper*? How could you watch that and not get a hard-on?"

It was a seminal moment—and I choose those words very carefully.

Of course, the object of my affections was not there on the day we were. There was just a show-off dolphin and a perky trainer in deck sneakers. I remember we'd missed the eleven o'clock show, but I insisted we wait for the next one, even though it meant standing for almost an hour in the ninety-five-degree heat. I *had* to stay just in case my favorite aquatic actor showed up. My parents, not knowing why I was so adamant about seeing the show, reluctantly obliged. Anything for their

Frankie
Goes to
Hollywood,
Fla.

73

little Frankie. By noon, the sun was excruciating, the heat unbearable. With each passing moment, my mother's patience grew thinner, melting away as fast as her pancake makeup.

"My girdle is burning my skin," Marian complained, taking off her big black sunglasses and mopping sweat from her brow with a tissue she'd pulled from her rattan handbag. Even her hair, which was always teased and lacquered with enough hair spray to withstand a hurricane, started to wilt.

"This show had better be good," she said.

Of course, it stank. It wasn't even the real Flipper.

"We're going back to the motel right now," Marian said, hot and beyond bothered, the moment that dolphin impostor did his last flip. "I'm going to take off my girdle and *let the fat fly!*" Which she did as soon as we got there. I went down the hall for ice while my father took out his travel bar and fixed her a Tom Collins. Along with a twenty-five-cent Magic Fingers mattress massage, it helped ease any lingering tensions behind the "Do Not Disturb" sign on Room 103, just off the parking lot near the pool.

We didn't return to Florida for several years after that. But in 1972, Grandma Carmela and her daughter Mary sponsored a bus trip there to benefit their church. My father refused to go because he hated buses, but he said we could go anyway. My mother and I didn't need any more encouragement than that. Although Carmela and Mary were not particularly experienced at running these trips, we signed up, along with almost three dozen Italian old people, most of whom could not speak English and dressed like the Dust Bowl version of *8½*. Nana agreed to go with us, and so did our neighbor, a blond divorcée named Vera who weighed eighty-six pounds. Her chubby red-haired son, Harold, came along too. He was seven years older than I chronologically but about five years less mature, so it evened out. He was a science fiction fanatic, rabid for Doc Savage novels and *Star Trek*.

Our trip together did seem like that TV show. It *was* as if we were going where no man had gone before . . . or at least where the bus driver had never gone before. The first night, after hours and hours on the road, he got lost and couldn't find our motel. We arrived at the motor lodge so late that all the restaurants in the North Carolina town had closed. Misfortune seemed to dog that bus. The next day, finally in Florida, the most elderly woman in the group, a saggy octogenarian with glasses like aquarium walls, tried carrying a twenty-pound bag of Indian River grapefruit by herself and tripped over a fluorescent orange curb. There she was in a blue housedress and knee-highs, sprawled on the blacktop surrounded by bright yellow citrus fruit. It was quite a sight. She hadn't broken anything, but somebody called an ambulance anyway. "What a stupid ox," Nana muttered, looking out the window from her seat in the second row. "This is going to make us late again tonight!"

While we waited for the paramedics that afternoon,

Grandma Carmela tried to entertain her aged troops by telling dirty jokes in Italian over the bus PA system. All Marian and Vera and Harold and I could make out was "sonnamabeech" at the end of every one, but Carmela would howl, almost not able to get the punch lines out without bursting into hysterics, and all the old ladies would laugh, too. Except, of course, for the old broad out on the pavement, who sat there in a daze with an ice cube wrapped in an embroidered handkerchief pressed to the growing lump on her forehead.

When we finally got to Miami Beach the day after that, we checked into the Delano Hotel, an art deco behemoth that was tarnished in those days but somehow still glamorous. We unpacked our shorts, striped T-shirts, bathing suits, and flip-flops, and settled into our room with its two double beds, blond wood furniture, and ancient black-and-white television. We vowed that afternoon that we would stay clear of our elderly busmates until it was time to go home. We pretended we were jet-setters, even though this was my first time staying overnight in a building that had an elevator.

It was also the first time I'd ever stayed at a hotel and not a motel, and it gave me my first taste of the lush life I wanted to lead. We had dinner every night in the hotel, while Vera, a bag of bones in a sundress, flirted with the gay waiters. One night, she asked for a little bit of ice cream for dessert, so Manuel, our favorite attendant, brought her a teaspoonful of butter pecan in a big parfait glass. He was so funny and so cute that I got all flustered whenever he came to the table, even though I was only ten.

We spent our afternoons shopping on Lincoln Road or escaping the heat into the coolness of a movie matinee. Harold and I saw *Skyjacked*, with Leslie Uggams as a stewardess who says "Screw you!" to her hostage-takers. I felt so grown-up seeing a movie that had such language in it. The following week they were getting Alfred Hitchcock's *Frenzy*, about a necktie strangler. I had pretended to hang myself with a green plastic jump rope one time when I was about seven, and my father got so mad, he cut it up into little pieces with a garden shears. So I didn't want to see that one.

It would have made me miss my jump rope too badly.

The one thing we didn't miss on that trip, sad to say, was my father. Well, we did miss the big lug a little bit. But with him not there, we had my mother's idea of fun instead of his, which I liked a lot better. This trip wasn't to a camper show or a sports hall of fame. It was a week in a semiglamorous hotel with a saltwater pool and a lounge act in the dining room every night. In Miami, I was my mother's date, quite content at not having to share her with any other man.

Late one evening, she took me and the gang to Wolfie's for a not-quite-midnight snack of corned-beef sandwiches and cream sodas. Playing all day, then dressing for dinner, then getting to eat *again* at a time when I normally would have been in bed was everything I wanted a vacation to be. It reminded me of the sign we always had hanging up in our garage that said "Everything I Like Is Either Illegal, Immoral, or Fattening." Those days felt like all three. It didn't matter that we were a lot closer to Hollywood, Florida, than Hollywood, California. That trip was like a tropical movie fantasy come true for me, my first taste of life as a bon vivant in white monk-strap dress shoes.

It gave me, too, a glimpse of my mother as she'd been in her youth, when she posed for souvenir photos, slim and immaculately dressed, against the leopard-print banquettes of Café Zanzibar in New York City, or jitterbugged on the dance floors of many a nightclub with suitors whose names she never mentioned. Her past, exposed over dinner on those nights in the ballroom of the Delano, gave me hope that my sophisticated dreams weren't so far-fetched that I might never realize them as the gay adult I was already itching to become.

L u s t
U n d e r
t h e
F o r s y t h i a

$\mathcal{I}$ should have known

I was not going to be a garden-variety heterosexual
that afternoon in first grade when Mrs. Pinney went
down the hall for a minute to see Mr. Yurkosky, the
principal who always told us, "It's spelled princi-
P-A-L because I'm your friend." I was standing by the
windows—the tilt-in kind with the manila-colored
shades that roll up from the bottom—checking my
spring project, marigold seedlings in milk cartons,
when the flat-topped, face-like-a-fist kid we called the
Knuckle did something very spontaneous and, to my
precocious little mind, wonderful.

He took one of those thick black pencils with no
eraser—the standard-issue ones that are perfect for
drawing a cloudy sky or writing three-line composi-
tions. But instead of using it to draw seagulls in

A
B o y
N a m e d
P h y l l i s

flight—that double arch against a setting circle sun—
or practice his cursive writing, which we were learning
at the time, the Knuckle tried to stick the blunt end
of it right through the seat of my brushed cotton chi-
nos like he was putting a candle in a birthday cake,
only the cake was me. Any other kid would have been
horrified and socked him good, but I wasn't, and
didn't. I *was* scared of this tough, belligerent kid, but
as much as he intimidated me, I liked him, too. So as
he shoved with all his might, my discomfort was
coupled with a stirring in my six-year-old loins—a
queasy-good, eyes-rolling-back, ouch-don't-stop! sort
of sensation that gay men dedicate their adult lives to
finding again and again.

The Knuckle could really have hurt me with his
primitive implement, I suppose, but that thought
never occurred to me. I was too caught up in the
brusque excitement of the moment. His pencil-
pushing, much to my dismay, was over a minute later
when Mrs. Pinney returned.

Home for lunch and puzzled by this first gleeful-
fearful quasi-sexual episode, I told my mother what
had happened. I figured she'd explain it. She explained
everything else, like why Grandpa spat in a can all the
time, and why Nana wore her stockings rolled like
doughnuts, and why Daddy looked like a gorilla when
he took his shirt off. I made the mistake, however, of
telling her that I *liked* being the human pencil sharp-
ener. She flipped. "Don't you ever let anyone try to

do something like that to you again!" she shrieked, her face as red as the mixture of Sun Bronze and Pink Silver dye in her hair.

So much for School #1's Head Start program in sodomy.

If she'd ever found out about my experience the following year with Van, one of the older boys I knew, she would have killed him and me, even though it was perfectly innocent compared with how sordid I wanted it to be. I'd been playing at his house all day long, which was fun because the place was spooky and old. But I was tired of trying on his sisters' injection-molded plastic wigs and playing Green Ghost and consulting the Magic 8 Ball. I was bored with the girls and their pet gerbils and playing hide-and-seek in the basement. So I went looking for Van. When I found him, he was up in his room doing what teenaged boys love to do. He was embarrassed that I caught him choking the chicken, but, at my urging, he continued. I'd never seen anything approaching adulthood—at least, not standing at attention—and I was bewitched. Compared to my prepubescence, his penis was the size of the Bullwinkle balloon in the Macy's Thanksgiving Day Parade, and, best of all, it was attached to a handsome olive-skinned boy with the blackest hair, above and below. Impressed by this newest part of him, I asked if I could feel it. "Well, okay," he said, rather reluctantly. "But gently." So I did. It was as soft as velvet, as hard as steel, and touching it gave me the

most magical sensation I'd felt in my single-digit years
on the planet.

"Don't you want to touch mine?" I asked before
long. He said no, which considering the fact that he
was a teenager, ten years older than me, was probably
wise. We'd both have been in shit with our parents,
but he'd *really* have gotten it handed to him. Still, I
felt terribly put out by his lack of reciprocity. What's
fair is fair, I thought. Just then, our moment together
was over. One of his sisters began climbing the nar-
row stairs that led to the second floor, one hand on
the banister, another on the faded forties floral-
wallpapered wall with its border of handprint smudges.
Panicked, Van tucked himself as best he could back
into his dungarees, which were only slightly less stiff
than he was. "Don't tell anyone about this," he
warned; his deep voice was hot breath upon my face.
I vowed in that moment of intimacy that I wouldn't
ever say a word—not even to Heidi, and I told her
everything.

Van's making me promise left me feeling that what
we had done, as harmless as it was, was somehow dirty,
which perplexed me. How could something so thrilling that it took my breath away be something we
weren't supposed to do? I knew I'd never be able to
resist the urge to duplicate the excitement I felt with
him and the Knuckle and the other boys with whom
I so innocuously experimented.

Even if it was the worst sin in the world, I was going to keep doing it.

My fascination with other boys resulted in a pattern of not–quite–coitus interruptus over the years. On summer afternoons when we were seven or eight, Joshua, the boy next door, and I would expose ourselves under the forsythia bushes between our houses. He'd take his out and I'd take mine out and we'd look at each other, but never touch. Why we didn't, I'll never know. When fall came and the foliage thinned, we feared that someone would see us touching ourselves, like the nosy kid across Second Avenue with the speech impediment, who said "hostible" instead of "hospital." He was always around. So we moved our practice to my father's tool closet in the garage. Climbing in among the shovels and pickaxes and ice choppers, we took our pants off and touched ourselves. My father, hearing a rustling in his tool closet, once tried to open the door, but I'd locked it from the inside. I knew this was something I shouldn't share.

"What are you doing in there?" he demanded.

"Playing," I said, pulling up my pants.

"Playing what?" he asked.

"Batman and Robin! This is the Batcave. You can't come in unless we knock you out with Batgas first," I said, thinking as fast as I could.

"Well, get out of there—you're going to hurt yourselves, for Christ's sake."

L u s t
U n d e r
t h e
F o r s y t h i a

83

We opened the door, a bit sheepishly, and never played that game again. One day, though, sitting on my neighbor boy's front porch waiting for him to come out and play, I turned to see him come down the stairs completely nude, a slight crook in the pink of his anatomy. Sun was streaming in through an upstairs window and bathing him in light. He was beautiful, like a vision to me. Arousing in a Lourdes kind of way, heaven right there on Prospect Street. When finally he came out, fully dressed, I didn't say a word about what I'd seen. I knew he wouldn't want to hear how turned on I was.

By the time we were ten, we boys explored our as-yet-ambiguous sexuality in other creative, clandestine ways. We flashed each other under the loop-stitched chenille covers at sleep-over parties. Once, at my urging, we pretended our genitals were models in a fashion show as we shone a flashlight/spotlight on them. I provided commentary, treating our dicks like Barbie dolls, saying "This ensemble is from the Paris collection . . ." Skinny-dipping at night in our backyard pool, we made deals: "I'll do a handstand and you watch, and then you do a handstand and I'll watch," knowing our lower halves would peek above the waterline in a moonlit game of "I'll show you mine, you show me yours." Getting caught in the rain and hiding in the upstairs closet, in underwear only, while our pants spun dry in the Kenmore, we would tug at each other, understanding nothing except that our parents would have a fit if they knew what we were doing.

Sexual expression, especially between boys, was not something they tolerated or understood. It was dirty and wrong, no matter how good it felt. "You're over-sexed!" my mother would say whenever I mentioned the subject. And, in our house, *any* interest in sex was deemed too much. My mother had little interest in it. "My *schmushke*'s dead," she'd say. To hear my grand-mother tell it, sex was something to be endured not enjoyed. And masturbation, well, that was just as bad. "Stop touching your *peeshadeel* or it'll fall off," she'd tell me. Like every boy, though, I thought taking my pants off was a *wonderful* activity. I used to love to hide underneath racks of dresses in Great Eastern Mills and expose myself. I would dare myself that I could unzip my pants, take out my *peeshadeel,* and not get caught by my mother or anyone else. I got a thrill out of that—which, thankfully, I have never sought to re-capture in my adult life at, say, Bergdorf Goodman. But the fear of discovery, always present in our house, is a powerful aphrodisiac.

There was so little privacy at home on Prospect—doors forbidden to be closed, parents who never went out at the same time, a grandmother who moved as silently as the Shadow and thought nothing of sneak-ing up on you—that the chance of discovery was al-ways good. Because of this, I learned to masturbate quickly and quietly—so quickly and quietly, in fact, that I once did it during a boring part of *The*

Hindenburg at Cinema 46 without ever letting my friend Lanz know what I was doing under the green nylon parka I'd tented over my lap. I relished those occasions when Nana went to see Papa Vic and my parents went to mass on Saturday night, when I'd finally have an hour to myself, but they were few and far between. Invariably, the phone would ring, interrupting my bliss, or the garage door would go up, signaling the early return of the Collection Plate Usher and the Rosarian, or of Nana, the fleet-footed four-foot-tall disrupter back from her son's house.

Pornography played a big role in my fantasy sex life. I had seen *Playgirl* at Heidi's house, thanks to her very hip mother. But I couldn't exactly buy one for myself in 1975. A twelve-year-old boy might be brave enough to buy *Playboy*, but *Playgirl*? Never. I knew, however, that every November *Playboy* had a feature called "Sex in Cinema," which always had naked men in it, too. I'd seen my first glimpse of a naked man in *Playboy*, a still from the film *The Naked Ape*. So I asked my father to buy me a copy for my next birthday. He did, thinking the sight of gatefolded female flesh wouldn't do his son any harm. But instead of the November issue, he came home with Miss October! The woman looked like Suzanne Somers with big pink nipples and hair the color of straw. She *did* turn me on, but I knew she wasn't what I really wanted. Men were what I so desperately wanted to see. In my hunger, I'd memorized every underwear ad in every magazine I could get my hands on—Jim Palmer in Elance briefs, Pete Rose in International Skants, an unknown pitcher in Scandia Mesh. In vain, I had pressed my face to the TV set during soap commercials, looking down the screen in an attempt to see the guy's penis. But that didn't work as well as I'd hoped.

Knowing he'd goofed and gotten the wrong issue, my father returned home with the November issue of *Playboy* as soon as it hit the stands. I gave October to Nana, who'd been asking to see it. She opened the centerfold and said *"Che scorno!"*—How shameful!— and then read the entire issue. I made off to my bedroom with Miss November '76 and that "Sex in Cinema" feature. Oh, to see porcelain-pale Jon Voight nude, with one leg up to shield himself from the camera, in *End of the Game*, hairy Harry Reems with pants around his ankles in a shot from *The Opening of Misty Beethoven*, Roger Mosley, coal black and glistening in *Drum*, the head of his manhood dangling a few inches lower than the white woman he was carrying in his arms. I was in ecstasy, thanks to *Playboy*, and my father never knew what thrills he'd handed over to me under the guise of heterosexual entertainment.

A year later, feeling brave enough to buy a copy of *Playboy* myself, I picked up the November 1977 issue. There was Rainbeaux Smith lying beneath six nude guys, a basketball team she agreed to service, a tangle of bodies all facedown except her, in *Slumber Party '57*. I so wanted to be that woman, minus the blue

87

A
B o y
N a m e d
P h y l l i s

eye shadow, to feel the weight of those men on me. And then, there was Nureyev, full frontal, in a scene from *Valentino*. He seemed so mysterious and yet so familiar—a gay man playing a straight one, like me in my room, alone with my magazines, listening to Meat Loaf singing "All Revved Up with No Place to Go."

These issues of *Playboy*, as happy as they made me, only whetted my appetite for *Playgirl*, with which I wouldn't need a magnifying glass to get a good glimpse of what I most wanted to see. In *Playboy*, the pictures of naked men had been so small. In *Playgirl*, I knew, they'd be front and center, if not as big as life. I re-membered that copy I'd pored over at Heidi's house years ago, and the centerfold a friend had found in the trash and given me when I was thirteen. My mother had found me with it and said I had to throw it away. Not wanting to waste a good thing, I put it in the mailbox on the corner because the mailman always seemed lonely and I figured he would like it. It didn't help him, though. One day, a few years later, we heard that he killed himself by putting his head down on the railroad tracks in Singac. His mother had died and he didn't want to live alone. He missed her too much.

Playgirl helped me through my loneliness, though, thank heaven. I used to sneak a peek at every new issue at the magazine stand near the checkout counter at the Valley Fair while my mother food-shopped. I used to hide *Playgirl* in a copy of *Mad* and pretend to be enraptured by Don Martin instead of someone named Derek or Matt. No one ever caught me. But it was awkward, trying to see every skin picture in the issue, not get caught by my mother or a manager, and keep my erection hidden from everyone else. Every month, I wanted to buy a copy, but every month I didn't have the nerve. When the February 1979 issue hit the stands, I had to own it, however. The Village People, who were my favorite disco group at the time, had posed seminude for a spread—the cowboy in only a wet tank top pulled down low; the construction worker in a jockstrap, the leather man with one gloved hand cupping his privates. I had to have this "veritable visual kaleidoscope of manhood," as they put it at *Playgirl.* Thank heaven for Donnie, my boss at my after-school job at Kaufman, the Carpet Experts, where I was a gofer.

He was a fifty-year-old salesman who was a cross between Liberace and Edward G. Robinson. Every afternoon, he filed his nails, which he kept long, and complained about what a shithole the store was. He was meant for bigger things and moved through life with a tremendous hauteur. He drove a navy-and-white Bill Blass signature Continental Mark IV, and lived with his mother in a house that had Greek statues in the 69 position in the garden. He was never open about his gayness, not at work, but it was obvious, at least to me. Wearing a toupee that made Burt Reynolds's look subtle, he referred to his live-in lover as

L u s t
U n d e r
t h e
F o r s y t h i a

89

his cousin and talked about sex with women in a voice that was like Jimmy Cagney with a splash of helium. I liked him and he liked me, mostly because we were both Italian, we both liked dirty jokes, and we both craved men. I asked him to buy me a copy of the magazine.

"You really want it?" he asked.

"I *have* to have it," I said.

"I'll bring it on Wednesday," he said. And he did.

When he arrived, he threw down a brown envelope on the desk we shared. It was taped shut. "Don't open it until you get home," he said. I wanted to leave right then. Fuck vacuuming carpet samples, picking up sandwich orders for the salesmen, and cleaning the bathrooms! I wanted to lock myself in my bedroom with the Village People. Eyeing the clock and thinking my shift would never end, I worked with more energy than usual. When the "Come In, We're Open!" sign on the front door got flipped to "Sorry, We're Closed," I grabbed my package, left with it under my arm, and hopped into my father's waiting car.

"I ate a sandwich, I'm exhausted, and I'm going right to bed," I said.

When I got home, I closed my bedroom door, took off all my clothes, got under the covers and opened the envelope. Donnie had thrown in not only the Village People issue, but that of the month before, plus copies of two magazines I'd not heard of before. One was called *Honcho*, the other *Mandate*; both were full

of hot, hairy men with mustaches to rival Anna
DeProspo's, and ads for "room odorizers," "personal
lubricants," and cottages in Key West with "swimsuit-
optional" swimming pools. A whole new world had
opened up for me.

A few years later, when I was in college and bold
enough to buy my own magazines—well, bold enough
to buy *After Dark*, anyway—I got some bad news. A
letter from one of my Kaufman's co-workers came saying Don had killed himself with an overdose of sleeping pills. My funny friend was yet another casualty of
time and place, and the inhospitable nature of the suburban environs we called home. By that time, the lust
I felt under the forsythia bushes, in tool closets or
upstairs bedrooms, or pawing through those now well-
worn copies of *Honcho* and *Mandate*, was something
I'd embraced. But, sadly, it proved too much for more
fragile souls, like Don and our postman and so many
nameless others, to handle.

Lust
Under
the
Forsythia

91

**A l l
B u t t
I m p o s s i b l e**

*A*t School #1, the
words I hated most—even more than "fag"—were
"skins versus shirts." I was invariably a "skin" at a time
in my life when I should have been a "shirt." Actually,
I should have been a "caftan" in 1970, but in Mr.
Brushcutz's phys. ed. class, that was not one of the
choices.

It would have saved me too much heartache.

I not only read more than any other kid in class
that year, but weighed more, too. My weight out-
stripped everyone's by the third grade, hitting triple
digits when other boys still weighed eighty-nine
pounds. I was fat but not really *that* big. No one
would have mistaken me for Totie Fields. But I was
chubby and carried it low—pear-shaped, like my
mother—which not only made getting an "A" in gym

quite improbable, but made wearing the regulation gym uniform all but impossible.

We were forced to wear these heavy twill gym shorts that we had to buy from the school. Mine never fit. They said "Extra Large" on the label, but I was Extra Larger. They were cut too high in the thigh, they pulled across the tush, and they rode right up into my crack if I so much as bent down to tie my high-tops. A wedgie was de rigueur, and if you didn't get one naturally, one of the boys would help you out, grabbing the back of your Fruit of the Looms and hiking them up to your shoulder blades. Chooch was notorious for this. He was a skinny little runt, with blond hair and green troublemaker eyes, who transferred from another school to ours in third grade and quickly made my misery his life's mission. The bane of my existence from grammar school to junior high, he would sneak up behind me and have me hanging off a locker hook before Mr. Brushcutz could even make it off the playground.

Of course, my regulation T-shirt never fit well, either. It was too tight and too short and emphasized the cleavage I was not supposed to have and the belly I couldn't get rid of. I not only *was* bad in gym, I *looked* like someone who was bad in gym—like "a fat bag of shit," as my father, God love him, once called me in a fit of anger.

Mr. Brushcutz offered no sympathy for my chubbiness or my inability to catch or kick a ball. With a silver flattop, heavy black glasses, and the thick but toned body of an Army commander, he was a Pep Boy look-alike, physically attractive in an Atomic Age sort of way. He would bark commands like "Arms up, move!" with all the mean-spirited relish of a neo-Nazi in shoes that pinch. He taught the boys. Miss Whitehead, who was so tall and so large that we called her Miss White House, taught the girls.

Mr. Brushcutz had an assistant, Mr. Kungle, who was totally cute and upon whom I developed a crush the day he arrived. He had hairy, muscled legs and an olive complexion that glistened with oil and sweat on the kickball yard. He was considerably younger than Mr. Brushcutz, and much nicer-looking. But he wasn't any more understanding of my inability to climb ropes, leap horses, or do flips on parallel bars that were barely wider than my hips. Mr. Kungle specialized in gymnastics, which he taught in the Apparatus Room, a high-ceilinged rectangle lit by row after row of fluorescent bulbs.

Glamour lighting, it wasn't.

The Apparatus Room was across the hall from where "Thumbs," an almost deaf man with enormous digits, taught "industrial arts": woodworking and metal shop. I was never any good at those activities either. The swordfish-shaped letter opener I made had a snout that was half an inch thick. My welding technique nearly blinded half the class. (I could never remember to say "Masks down!" before I sent sparks

95

flying.) And I couldn't go near the circular saw without imagining that wedgie-puller Chooch strapped to it, ready to be sawed in half, like the Riddler tried to do to Robin on *Batman*. I wanted to hurt that kid bad, but in shop class I only managed to hurt myself. I barely escaped alive.

There was one week when we traded with the girls. They took shop while the boys took home economics. A whiz in the kitchen, I was happy to make the switch, cooking up a one-dish ground-beef-and-olive Bisquick pizza that the kids loved. I was too good at home ec., in fact, which only fueled Chooch's verbal attacks. I was proud of my back-of-the-box culinary wizardry, though, and after school that day I told Lois about my experience. I figured she'd be impressed, since she was such a bad cook, and hoped she'd have some soothing words to smooth over how sissified the other kids made me feel. Instead she told me a joke.

"Knock, knock," she said.

"Who's there?"

"Bisquick."

"Bisquick who?"

"Bisquick your pants are on fire!" she said, giggling. It helped.

But even Lois couldn't save me from the pain of gym class.

If tools had been my enemy in shop, the ropes were my tormentors in Mr. Brushcutz's class. No matter how hard I tried to climb them, I couldn't lift my

103-pound body off the floor. I would wait in line for my turn, knowing I would never be airborne of my own volition. My stress level would rise as each kid climbed the thick wheat-colored rope, gave the ceiling a victory slap, and then came down hand over hand as fast as possible. When it came time for me, my heart would pound as I grabbed the rope in my hands. I'd huff and puff and strain trying to lift myself, but I just couldn't. I could feel the impatience of the thinner and more able-bodied kids, their gazes, searingly judgmental, on my back. My efforts vain, I'd let go of the ropes, turn with my head bowed, step off the foam mat, and go to the back of the line.

I really was a failure at physical education. Although I was a straight-A student otherwise, I never got more than a B in gym. If only there had been remedial gym classes for klutzes! In English, if you were a nimrod and didn't know that "a lot" is two words, you could get all the catch-up help in the world. But if you couldn't slam-dunk anything but a doughnut, you and your incredible shrinking self-esteem were made, time and again, to prove just how bad you were at balls—kick-, soft-, basket-, and dodge-.

No one was worse than me. In kickball, I'd always pop-fly, and before I could hustle my rotund little body to first base, someone would catch it and I'd have to make that U-turn of defeat and go back to the dugout. In softball, I wasn't much better, striking out

with alarming frequency. One day, though, I got up to bat determined to prove myself something other than a total spaz. The first pitch went right by me. I didn't even swing. "Strike one," Mr. Brushcutz said. The second pitch I swung at and missed. "Strike two," he said. But on the third pitch, I swung with all my might, and for once, my bat connected with the ball. It went farther than any other kid's hit had that day. I was dumbfounded, as surprised at what I'd done as Mr. Brushcutz was to see me do it. "Run, run!" he shouted. And, I did, circling the bases as fast as I could, not caring that I was sweating and out of breath and had a pain in my side from running so fast. I'd hit a home run.

No one could believe it, least of all me. I was a hero for about ten seconds until Chooch sneered, all wormlike evil, "You're still a fag 'cause it'll never happen again." He stole my happiness with one slur. Chooch knew I could never repeat that home run, and so did I.

The only thing worse than the constant humiliation of playing games in gym was having to take a shower with the other boys afterwards. A fat gay kid, nervous that his butt is too big and everything else is too small, knows no greater hell than being in a shower room surrounded by naked boys and not being able to enjoy it. I was nearsighted, and it was a good thing. If I had gotten a serious glimpse of my classmates and popped a boner it would have been a disaster. To make sure that didn't happen, I would fill my mind with disgusting images. Dead poodle puppies. Nuns with spears through their heads. Pieces of Wonder Bread soaking in the bottom of a urinal. Anything to remain unenthusiastic about the fact that I was in a steamy, tiled room full of naked boys. It worked. Thank heaven.

By the time I was fourteen, when puberty had reared its ugly head, I had something else to be self-conscious about when I was in the showers. By then, I was not only heavier than most of the boys, I was hairier, too. I'd inherited my father's genes, which meant that naked, I looked like I was wearing a mohair cat suit. Roddy McDowall in *Planet of the Apes* had nothing on my father. Robin Williams had nothing on me. I was a baby bear who had no idea that there were people who actually *liked* body hair. Certainly, I hated mine, thanks to my mother, who made it quite clear to me how ugly she thought it was. I was standing at the bathroom sink brushing my teeth one morning when she grabbed a yellow terry washcloth, stuck it under the running tap, and then tried *rubbing* the hair off my forearms. She was determined, despite my cries of "Ouch!" But when her depilatory methods showed little result, she sighed, "Oh, God, you're going to be just like your father." She had no idea how much damage those words did. It would be years before I felt comfortable again in my own fur.

In high school health class, where such changes in

our bodies were supposed to be explained to us, the teachers offered no advice and certainly no comfort. I wasn't surprised—they were gym teachers for three-quarters of the year. Why in God's name they were given the task of teaching health class too is beyond me. But they did. Sex education was the real shocker. It was taught by the same man who taught weight lifting, a big fat Italian guy with a thick head of black hair atop a pudgy face. He was named Big Steve, and possessed all the sensitivity of a pit bull with hemorrhoids. He had a mouth like one, too, swearing a blue streak and daring kids to report him. In sex ed., I prayed that he wouldn't get to the chapter in our textbooks on homosexuality. But he did, and it was truly amazing.

"I can't tell you what to think about ho-*mo*-sexuals," he said, pacing in front of the class, a barrel-chested *chidrool* in a kelly-green golf shirt with a little hornet embroidered where the crocodile should be. "Personally, I think they should shoot the bastards. But read this chapter and we'll talk about it next week." I couldn't wait. This was going to be something.

The following week, he began the class by handing out a true-or-false survey about sexual stereotypes, including gay ones, and asked us all to fill it out silently. He would wait while we did. There were statements about blacks and Asians and one that said "Homosexuals are more creative," which tickled me no end. I was still mad about his die-faggot proclamations the week before, so I went up to him with my paper and pointed to that line and said: "Do you mean *sexually* more creative, or in general?"

He looked at me, mean as all get-out, and snarled, "In general."

When he collected the papers, he asked, "Is there anyone in here who hasn't met a ho-*mo*-sexual?" Glaring at me, he said: "I'm sure we've got one or two in here, too." (We had four, actually, and that wasn't counting girls.) Cyn, a straight girl who later went on to Bible college, raised her hand and said she had not. I got a look on my face like "Is she kidding?" She knew *me*. What was she talking about? But gayness was invisible to her and to many of our classmates. Gays were freakish others, not kids sitting beside them. Those who knew we existed targeted us for their hate. The teacher, big fat Italian Steve, didn't do us gay boys any favors with his health class lessons, or any service to the lesbians, who were among the toughest and best athletes in the school. He spread intolerance, followed by lectures on how not to get pregnant before graduation. I hated him, but did nothing. I never reported him to the superintendent or told my parents how his hate lectures made me feel. How could I? To do that would be to admit that I was gay . . . and I was not yet prepared to stand up and tell everyone. Instead,

feeling like an alien in the most familiar of surroundings, misshapen and beleaguered, I suffered in silence.
I was good at that by then. I'd had lots of practice in
grammar school and junior high, thanks to Chooch
and a handful of others.

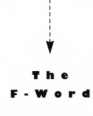

The
F-Word

*I*f you had any form
of mental or learning disability—or just a short attention span and bad eyewear—you ended up in Mrs.
Entwistle's class. She taught the "retards," as we so
sensitively called the dozen or so "special ed." children
at School #1 in the 1970s. Even those of us at the
other end of the special ed. spectrum, in the advanced-
placement classes, called them that. They were excep-
tional and so were we, but that didn't make us any
more understanding of their predicament, or they of
ours.

Mrs. Entwistle's classroom was hidden behind the
principal's office, next to the nurse, Mrs. Paullus,
whose last name, I was convinced, meant penis. (I confused it with "phallus.") The classroom was secluded
enough that we didn't have to see those kids much

103

during the school day, except when Jerry the Spaz de-livered half-pint milk cartons for snack, or when Con-fessor, the one black kid in the school, wheeled a projector to Miss Whitehead's girls-only health class, so she could show a film that had stuff in it that none of us boys were supposed to know about. In the name of education, the retards served as unpaid labor, se-questered from us "normal" children, except when do-ing menial tasks to enhance our learning experience.

But Mrs. Entwistle had one student none of us could ignore—a brown-haired, wiry little boy with a speech impediment and an all-gums smile that was so exuberant you had to adore him. His name was Jimmy, but when he said it, it sounded like Dimmy. Whenever he saw me in the hall, or rode his bike down Prospect past our house to go see his cousin Rosemary, he'd always yell "Hi, Fang!" as if I were Phyllis Diller's husband, and wave and wave with all his might until I saw him and waved back.

He was a sweetheart—a little embarrassing to know sometimes, but a sweetheart. Gentle and funny and a little weird in a neighborhood that didn't want for strangeness, Dimmy was a flouncy-bouncy addition to the after-dinner parade that passed by our front porch every night. Sitting at Nana's knee, I'd watch as the Twins, an identical twosome, crewcut and lithe, would walk by in unison, their synchronized steps in perfect formation. Then we'd spot Mrs. Dodawitch and her dachshund, Fritzie, who kept getting hit by cars but never died. Once in a while, Heidi's father, Don, would zoom by on his motorcycle, an orange helmet, a khaki windbreaker, and white socks and Hush Puppies where biker boots should have been. Dimmy was the star, though, a smiling trouper riding and waving as if taking a curtain call after a bravura performance of a play only he acted in.

Every year, on the day when the shipment of yearbooks arrived from the printer, the teacher would pass them out to all of us who'd ordered them and we'd get our classmates, even the ones we didn't like, to sign them. Moses, the Puerto Rican kid down the street, would always write "Bad luck, Moses." Joshua signed his "Good luck with Heidi!" No one ever asked Dimmy for his autograph, though. Everyone would have made fun of you if you did, especially Chooch. From the day he arrived, to make sure he wasn't picked on himself, he tortured any kid more defenseless than he was—which, at School #1, meant me and Dimmy. Until the seventh grade, that is, when a nerdy kid named David arrived, thank heaven. He became my friend and Chooch's biggest target. But that was later.

To Chooch, it didn't matter if you were a retard like Dimmy or a smart kid like David or me. If you weren't in the great teeming middle—because you were fat or gay or, heaven forbid, a *non-straight* straight-A student—you were marked. A "Kick Me Hard" sign would be on your back for what seemed like forever. It would be the last thing those kids saw when you left town, years down the road, when you'd had enough of being the brunt of every anti-queer joke, when you started to chart your own life and reclaim all that had been taken from you over the years, piece by piece, on otherwise average days. But who thought that day would ever really come? Certainly not me, not at School #1.

On one of those new-yearbook afternoons, I left class to go to the boys' room for just a few minutes and came back to find my fresh new copy of the yearbook not in my incredibly neat flip-top desk where I'd left it, but on top of it and opened. On Dimmy's picture, someone had written in fake retard scrawl, "Fang, member all duh good times, Dimmy." I wanted to cry when I saw it, a sore-throat lump developing instantly and growing more painful as I realized every kid had seen it while I was gone and had laughed, not at Dimmy but at me. Chooch had struck—a good blow, too. It was one of his more creative efforts. Usually, he just used the F-word.

Chooch—and, later, a handful of others—called me a faggot every weekday from the day he arrived through my junior year of high school. I got snow days and holidays off, of course, but this *was* a daily ritual. Sometime between eight-forty-five A.M. and three P.M. every day, someone would call me a faggot. "Queer" and "fairy" were used occasionally, too, and "wussy" was big for a while. But "faggot" (and, to save time, "fag") was the favorite of my tormentors. They had not heard of "poofter," "nancy boy," "big nellie," "major queen," "pillow biter," "butt buddy," or (my favorite) "dick smoker" in Little Falls in those days of Wacky Packages and *Bowling for Dollars*.

Chooch and company used the word "faggot" to mean not "homosexual" but "weakling" or "misfit" or "nerd." Whatever it was, it was the worst thing you could possibly be. Joshua, the little tough guy I used to play doctor with in the forsythia bushes, used the word whenever someone punched him or hit him with a snowball. His face would turn beet-red, like he was going to burst a vein in his head, he'd say, "Now you die, faggot!," and then he'd clobber them. "Faggot" just meant you weren't cool.

I certainly wasn't. Even if I'd been heterosexual, I would still have been a faggot in Chooch's eyes. I had the best marks in the class and racked up certificates of merit at the annual awards assembly the way black cashmere gathers lint. Teachers didn't do us smart kids any favors. They singled us out as examples, asking the other children, "Why can't you be more like him?" or saying, "*This* is what a book report is supposed to sound like" and then having you read it out loud, thereby making us pariahs, magnets for all the hatred that preteens could muster.

"They're just jealous," my mother would say.

But of what I was never sure.

There were days when the big event was getting hit

A
B o y
N a m e d
P h y l l i s

in the head with a wad of clay the size of a baseball or getting kicked in the face on the jungle gym and getting sent home with a black eye that turned out to be more shoe polish than anything else. Both hurt like hell, of course, but I did nothing to exact revenge. I just waited for it all to end. Somehow I knew it would. I just hoped I'd live long enough to see that day.

The worst experience involved a kid named Keenan. He was a tough blond kid with a lisp—go figure—who made out with older girls in the hallway of school when most of us were still only interested in playing with our Captain Action dolls and watching reruns of *Lost in Space*. He spat on me, just for the fun of it, one day. He pegged me good with a big green loogie on the back of my parka, drawing the mucus up from his lungs and really letting me have it. It was the most degrading thing that happened to me in all my years in Little Falls, unless you decide that words can hurt just as much as a saliva shower or a Kiwi Brand shiner.

In Mrs. Reed's seventh-grade art class, I made a giant three-dimensional initial "F" out of cardboard and painted it with optic-yellow and electric-blue polka dots. It was what Mary Tyler Moore's "M" would have looked like if she had lived downstairs from H. R. Pufnstuf instead of Rhoda. It was a good "F," if I say so myself, and the teacher held it up to show everyone. When she did, Chooch said "What's the 'F' for? 'Faggot'?" Everyone laughed in one big collective fit, but the teacher did nothing, except tell the class to quiet down, which they did when they were quite through giggling. After class, she took me aside and said, "Don't let those kids bother you." But how could I not let them bother me? I'd made the best project of anyone and was still the laughingstock of School #1. And, besides, what he called me was what I was. Even Mrs. Reed knew I was a future homo.

Today, of course, I could tell Chooch to his face what the F really stands for: "Fuck you!" But back then I was devastated. I thought, How can I defend myself against such a hateful word when what he's saying ultimately is true? I mean, I'd known I was gay since the day in kindergarten when we made plaster molds of our right hands and I screamed because I was afraid mine would get stuck and I'd never be able to wear long sleeves again. Actually, that's not true. The *other kids* had known I was gay since that day in kindergarten. *I* figured it out in my junior year of high school, when I fell in love with a boy from my geometry class, the boy who would not only become my first boyfriend but would nickname me Phyllis. By then, when I actually *was* engaging in homosexual activity, the kids had stopped calling me faggot, oddly enough. I had become popular by then, but even that wasn't roses.

It was years before I could hear the word "faggot" uttered by or about anyone without feeling mortally wounded and being mentally transported back to the art class where I made that fucking "F." Thank heaven that, as adults, we've taken back all those evil words that were hurled at us in our youth. We've embraced them, wearing "Big Fag" or "Dyke University" T-shirts, and jokingly referring to each other as nancy boys or bulldaggers. In their way, these fashion statements take the sting out of our very painful pasts. They help us live in the present, when the threats to our lives are a lot more dangerous than Chooch or Keenan.

I thought I would never hear the word "faggot" again after I left Little Falls, and for the most part I didn't. But in 1985, when I interviewed for my first big job—as a menswear columnist at the *Detroit Free Press*—the hiring editor, a woman to whom the home perm was the single greatest invention since fire, took me to lunch. It was one of those big, dark, clubby men's restaurants with red banquettes and Cobb salad on the menu and lots of men in dark suits and comb-over haircuts. A restaurant she thought had real character. I hate places like that.

Anyway, before our entrees had arrived, she cut to the chase. She asked how I felt about the "faggot factor" of the job, and my jaw nearly hit the table. "The what?" I asked. "Well," she explained rather gingerly, "a male fashion writer is immediately assumed to be gay. Can you handle that?"

I knew I could—I mean, *hello!*—but I didn't know

what to say. I wasn't *out* out then; I was just out to my chums and my family and, of course, the occasional boyfriend. So, I thought, Do I tell her the whole truth and let the chips fall where they may? Or should I just be clever and not say more than I need to? For better or worse, I chose clever.

"Well, Joan," I said, "I've never done typical *boy* things. Little League didn't pan out for me. I flunked knot-tying in Webelos. So, what I'm trying to say is, I really don't think the 'faggot factor' will be a problem for me."

She didn't know I'd heard that word five days a week for nine years.

In 1993, when I was working for *New York Newsday*, I sat on a panel of openly gay columnists at the National Lesbian and Gay Journalists Association convention and told the story about my *Detroit Free Press* interview lunch. A gay reporter covering the discussion for the organization's newsletter later wrote that, along with other openly gay journalists, I had *become* the faggot factor at my newspaper. "Damn straight," was all I could think to say. But that was when I was thirty-one, not thirteen.

At thirteen or fifteen or even twenty, I wasn't comfortable with being openly gay, not like now, even though I'd always put the "boy" in "flamboyant" as a child. But I never really wished I were straight, even though it would have made my life a lot easier. Not even when facing Chooch's hate or being pushed around by a couple of tough kids from my high school homeroom, burnouts from Totowa who smoked dope before class. Every morning, they would stand in front of my locker and not let me get to it. They'd push me around like a punching bag and make me drop my books, or try to burn me with a cigarette lighter one of them always carried.

These straight kids who called us faggots hated us, but they were terrified of us even more, I think. They'd been brought up to believe that being gay was the worst thing you could possibly be. We all were taught that. Even the most tolerant kids didn't want to be gay. One day in my senior year in high school, I was sitting in the quiet section of the library, studying. Gary, the class president, was sitting a few carrels away, doing whatever it is class presidents do during a free period. I noticed that Dimmy had appeared, walking into the library happy as could be. He spotted Gary the All-American, but Gary didn't see him. Dimmy snuck up behind him, wrapped his arms around the BMOC, began rubbing his sides, and said loud enough for everyone to hear, "I wuv you Gawwy! You wuv me, too?" Gary jumped up, eyes as wide as saucers, horrified by this public display of affection, looking as if he'd just been sodomized. I thought he was going to scream. I'd never seen "homosexual panic" before, but it was hilarious. This gentle soul had terrified a football quarterback. Dimmy—not gay, just aflush with puberty—was my hero that day.

Flamboyant
Like
Me

*L*ike every girl in
America, when *The Partridge Family* premiered in
1970, I developed an instant crush on David Cassidy.
As Keith, the singing-est family's oldest boy, he was
so sexy with his long hair and tight bell-bottoms, and
those polyester shirts that he wore unzipped practically
to his navel. Of course, like every prepubescent gay
boy in America, I told everyone I had a crush on Susan
Dey, who played his sister Laurie, instead.

It was what I thought I was supposed to have, but
didn't.

In the fifth grade, after *The Partridge Family* had
been on a couple of years, I bragged to Mrs.
Hagman—the "hippie teacher," as Marian called her,
who'd come to us from a Montessori school and
brought plenty of progressive (and progressively more

unwelcome) ideas with her—that if I had one wish, it would be to have Susan Dey for twenty-four hours.

"Twenty-four hours, huh? What would you do with her?" she asked.

"I don't know," I answered sheepishly. "Play games . . . color?"

I was so embarrassed, getting caught at ten in midleer not knowing a thing about sex and having a grown-up call my bluff. It was dumber than the time I ruined my school picture in Miss Gioia's third grade. My mother had dressed me up in a hound's-tooth blazer and combed my hair into a tiny modified pompadour with a rat-tail teasing comb and some ancient styling gel she'd saved from her beauty shop. That morning, I was more kempt than anyone for blocks and really ready for my close-up. But when the school photographer sat me down in front of the camera, his finger on the shutter button, he shouted, "Say 'I like girls'!" not "Say 'Cheese'!" Instead of smiling, I burst out laughing, a little bit of snot coming out of my nose as I tried to stifle my giggling fit. In a flash, he caught it all.

Even in the wallet photo, I looked ridiculous.

When it came to girls, I *did* like Laurie Partridge, though, with her ax-parted hair and her penchant for women's lib rallies. But I *loved* Keith. He was my main man—the dreamiest dreamboat on a dream night of TV. Parked in front of our new nineteen-inch Panasonic color set, my brushed-denim butt on the speckled carpet with the white flecks that I once tried to color in with permanent Magic Marker (I got in big trouble), I lived for *The Brady Bunch*, *The Partridge Family*, *Room 222*, and *The Odd Couple*. For a while there *Nanny and the Professor* was in the mix, too. If I could keep my eyes open long enough on those Friday nights to watch *Love, American Style*, I would sit enthralled by the fireworks of that risqué "late night" TV show, while Marian read the *Newark Star Ledger* and Frank Senior snored on the couch. That was my weekly delight, my night with Keith, a refuge from everything that was bugging me in the real world.

Over the years, I figured the best way to worship my teen-god idol was to collect as much Partridge Family stuff as I could. I bought every Partridge Family record as soon as it came out, plunking down $2.99 for each one on sale at Tops. *The Partridge Family Album*, *Up To Date*, *Sound Magazine*, *Shopping Bag*, and even *A Partridge Family Christmas Card*, which was mottled green and white and came with an actual holiday greeting from their house to ours—I got them all.

At fifty cents a pop, I bought *Tiger Beat* and *Sixteen*. I treasured the one whose cover promised a "Huge Sizzling Giant All-Color Room-Size David Cassidy Pull Out Poster Free Inside!" I bought volume after volume of Partridge Family mystery novels, the lunch box, and then the trading cards—first the yellow set, then the blue, searching pack after pack for the

F l a m -
b o y a n t
L i k e
M e

115

A
B o y
N a m e d
P h y l l i s

elusive "Keith Spruces Up!" card. And, at lunch and dinner, I drank enough grape Hi-C for ten children and saved the labels so I could send away for a set of five-by-seven Partridge Family glossies. When the postman brought them, I was in orbit.

As if that weren't enough merchandise, I bought a six-foot, big-as-life poster of David Cassidy in a white-fringed jumpsuit—a Keith Partridge–as–skinny–Elvis kind of thing. He looked so delicious with his "groovy physique," as they said in that "David's Secret Love Tricks!" article I'd read in *Sixteen*. I hung the poster on the wall next to my door. I liked to imagine he was coming into my bedroom to rescue me from the doldrums of Prospect Street. I fantasized that David would adopt me and we would go on the road together in that Mondrian-style bus of his. I would be his ward, like Dick Grayson was Bruce Wayne's on *Batman*. We would be a dynamic duo, too, I figured.

Daydreaming as I listened to his records, I would swoon when he did his rap in the middle of "Doesn't Somebody Want to Be Wanted." So breathily I wanted to scream, he'd say how lonely it was on the road and ask, "Now where is love and who is love, I gotta know."

"David, love is right here. It's me," I wanted to say, but I couldn't.

My parents didn't see anything wrong with my blatant affection for the hunkiest Partridge, or with the strange fact that their son identified not with Danny

Partridge, the little red-haired wheeler-dealer of the family, who was about my age, but with Reuben Kincaid, the group's manager, who was old enough to be my father. It had been the same for me with *The Brady Bunch.* I always felt like Alice the maid, not Peter or Bobby. And when I watched *H. R. Pufnstuf,* I wanted to be the evil Witchiepoo with her souped-up Broom-Broom and striped stockings, not Jimmy, the little boy with the bell-bottom trousers and the magic flute. My parents always said I was "ten going on forty," and treated me like the funny featured player in the situation comedy of their lives. So that's the part I played: the miniature adult. In retrospect, I was a little boy just *screaming* for therapy. But no one heard my cries.

When Bobby Sherman's show *Getting Together* premiered in 1971, I developed a crush on him, too. As soon as it came on, I became sold on *his* groovy physique and *his* love of fringed jumpsuits. Bobby was just too cute, with a Colgate smile and a leather choker, and even my father liked his hit song "Julie, Do Ya Love Me." Although I still watched *The Partridge Family,* David Cassidy became old news after Bobby appeared. I took to writing "Super Dope" on pictures of my once-beloved shag-haired honey in my copy of *Tiger Beat's Official Partridge Family Magazine.*

Bobby was cooler than David—who really was smug, when you got right down to it—because on *Getting Together,* Bobby was secure enough to have a nerdy best friend named Lionel Poindexter. Lionel wasn't the cutiepie that Bobby was. He was an attractive oddball, only he didn't know he was attractive. And he drove a hearse. I was at least ten years younger than he was, but I identified with him. I already knew I was never going to be David or Bobby, but I might be Lionel. I already was a "Poindexter." All I needed was a hearse and maybe I'd be a cool nerd, too. Maybe people like Bobby and David might like me then. Bobby's friendship with Lionel made it seem okay to be different, helped me believe that it wasn't the worst thing in the world not to blend in. You could be an eccentric and still have friends, not to mention a fabulous "car."

But all that was kid stuff. When Elton John released "Crocodile Rock" in 1973, my life changed forever. In him, I found the role model I'd been looking for, and he wore marabou feathers, pink satin suits, and platform shoes. Elton gave me hope that I could survive a blitzkrieg of insults from kids like Chooch and any other indignities Little Falls might hold for me. No one made me happier.

I didn't have a crush on Elton John so much as I wanted to *be* him or at least play him in the movie *The Elton John Story* that I fantasized they'd make someday. So in the sixth grade, when I couldn't see the blackboard in Mrs. Little Green Sprout's class and found out that I had to wear glasses, I was thrilled. Being nearsighted made me more like my hero, a balding piano player who dressed like no man I knew, except for Liberace, whose records my grandmother played on her GE phonograph while she baked eggplant parmigiana and knocked back a few Millers.

"Crocodile Rock" was the first single I ever bought that wasn't stupid. In Miss Hehn's music appreciation class at School #1, when it was my turn to transcribe song lyrics onto mimeo paper, so she could run them off and everyone could sing along, I picked that song.

Miss Hehn was not a pleasant woman. Gangly and tall, with dyed brown hair messily piled on top of her head, she looked like Ichabod Crane in drag and said, "Soft-pedal it, you fresh articles!" whenever we got out of hand. We called her Chicken Legs behind her back. Pushing sixty and believing life had been better when Percy Faith ruled the airwaves, she was ill-equipped for ten-year-olds who worshiped Kiss. Chooch drove her crazy by sticking his tongue out as far as it would go and doing Gene Simmons impressions while playing air guitar.

I played air piano on my desk, pretending to be Elton. In July 1975, Michael Hughes stole for me his father's copy of *Time* with "Rock's Captain Fantastic" on the cover, and the more I learned about Elton John, the more I liked him. A month later, Elton was on the cover of *People* wearing gold aviators with palm trees on them. Oh, how I wanted those glasses! Inside was a portrait of Elton in a cropped tank top, exposing his hairy tummy, and satin short shorts, the outline of his penis apparent through the shiny material. He was standing in a giant walk-in closet with hundreds of pairs of platform shoes at his feet. The picture turned me on, not only because of its anatomical suggestiveness but because of the shoes. This was the man I wanted to be—at least, throughout my early teens.

When Elton announced in *Rolling Stone* that he was bisexual, I felt an instant kinship with him that I'd never really felt with anyone else, even though I wasn't exactly sure what "bisexual" meant. I just knew it made him different. Elton, more sensitive than the typical rock star, was someone whose childhood dreams were quashed by a home life ill-suited to his artistic temperament. His father didn't understand him any better than mine did me. I knew that. He was living out his childhood fantasies in his adult life. That was what I planned to do, too. Elton was excessive and impulsive and terribly glamorous. He had furs and the nerve to wear them.

No man ever had such courage in Little Falls.

Heidi adored Elton John, too. We had to have every new album of his the day it came out. We would have died if we didn't. Heidi and I made Marian drive to the Sam Goody at Wayne Hills Mall three days in a row trying to get copies of *Captain Fantastic and the Brown Dirt Cowboy*, Elton's autobiographical album, when it was released in the summer of 1975. It never dawned on any of us that you could call to find out if it was there or not.

But schlep, my mother did.

When we heard Elton was going to play the Pinball Wizard in *Tommy*, we were beside ourselves. We didn't know who the director, Ken Russell, was (or who the *Who* was, for that matter) but we loved the movie and Elton's enormous Doc Marten boots. Crazy for his diamanté glasses and that Lurex cap he wore with the silver ball on the top of it, I took shirt cardboard from my father's dresser drawer, and glitter that my mother had picked up at Lee Wards, and, with Elmer's Glue, made clip-on silver sparkle glasses to attach to my own. With them, I wore a blue cap that Nana had knitted for me with a Christmas ball pinned to the top. It wasn't exactly the Pinball Wizard, but it was close enough. My dresser top became my keyboard as I played along to all his 45s; my bedroom mirror, my audience of adoring fans.

Elton was a guest star on the first *Cher* show in February 1975. That night, he sang not only with Cher, who was so chic in those days you could die, but with the woman whom I (like every other gay boy of that era) most idolized—Bette Midler. Midler, for me, was like the female Elton. She wasn't beautiful, but she was fabulous. And her parents were from Paterson, New Jersey—where my grandmother grew up! What was not to love? When Bette's Cleveland concert was on HBO twenty-three times in one month, I watched every single telecast. She was so naughty, and she quoted Belle Barth, a "vulgarian" comic whose blue records my mother adored. Cher had Flip Wilson on her special, too. Marian and I always loved his show, especially his drag character, Geraldine, who once said, "You don't have to be a thing of beauty to be a joy forever." I loved that idea.

For the *Cher* show finale, all four of them—Bette, Elton, Flip, and Cher—wore white costumes covered in rhinestones, glitter balls, and mirror tiles, and performed surrounded by a sea of white balloons. That number was the most glamorous thing I'd ever seen in my life. I wanted to live in a world where such a thing was possible, where so much talent and so much fabulousness could coexist. At the time, I couldn't imagine I would ever get to see any of them in the flesh.

I never dreamt that by the time I was thirty-two, I'd have met all of them. Not surprisingly, none impressed me more than Elton. When I met him—backstage at a Gianni Versace fashion show in Milan in 1994—I told him just how much inspiration he gave me and so many others. "You don't know how much you meant to all of us," I said. "You gave us strength and courage . . . even before you came out. You told us it was okay to be ourselves." He got teary-eyed as I gushed. I could have just gone on and on. Instead I said, "You know, I've waited twenty-two years for this moment and now I'm going to have a heart attack standing here talking to you." He laughed, said, "Don't be silly," and gave my arm a squeeze.

Some gay men say that, as children, they wanted

to kill themselves because the only gay people they ever saw were flamboyant queens like Elton John. But for me, outrageous, bigger-than-life characters—whether they were really queer or just playing gay—made me want to be gay. Whether it was David Bowie in a dress, flanked by drag queens Klaus Nomi and Joey Arias, singing "Boys Keep Swinging" on *Saturday Night Live* in 1979, or John Hurt playing the lavender-haired British eccentric Quentin Crisp in the movie *The Naked Civil Servant* on PBS, they gave me the promise of a life more colorful than the one I knew. I didn't want to be a drag queen, I just wanted the nerve to be myself. I wanted a share of the gumption they had to spare.

On a talk show once, one of my favorite people, Charles Nelson Reilly, told a story about being invited to ride a float in a Gay Pride parade. He'd been told the float would say "Actors for Gay Rights"—which he had no problem with—but when he got there, it turned out to say "Gay Actors for Human Rights." No one would get on the float, he said. But he had put on his tux and his toupee and he looked good and he was going to do it. So he got on the float. Unfortunately, when the news crews saw that it was only him up there among the tissue-paper flowers, they turned off the cameras. "You couldn't come out on TV if you wanted to," he complained. Really, if Reilly—a man who had played the Bic Banana and once provided the "voice behind the fruit" of a gelatin dessert—was riding a Gay Pride float, who cared? Well, I did.

Flamboyant people like him and Paul Lynde, Liberace, and Divine made me glad to be gay. They were funny and over-the-top. And, more than anything, they were their glorious selves at a time when most of us were afraid *just to be*. Oh, sure, they fueled stereotypes of gay men, but they had style to spare. People may have laughed at Liberace's hot pants and Paul Lynde's caftan all those years ago, but these characters provided larger-than-life liberation from the beigeness of convention for all of us Technicolor kids growing up in suburbia. By shining example, they offered a *way-out* way out for those of us who didn't want to be stereotypical, but just turned out that way. Swishy hairdressers, show-tune queens, fashion designers, and me—someone who was outed in kindergarten.

Elton John gave me the strategy I've used throughout my life. He made it clear to me that I could reinvent myself, as he had done, taking my natural flamboyance and running with it. He didn't deny who he had been in his childhood—the unhappy, misunderstood youth named Reginald Kenneth Dwight; he transcended it and truly became Elton Hercules John. He took the effeminacy that his schoolmates derided him for and sold it back to them as fabulousness. More than anything, he proved that you could be yourself, get paid for it, and maybe—just maybe—get the

Keith Partridge of your dreams, too. I hoped I would be so lucky.

In 1977, however, I temporarily forsook my hero. I traded Elton John for John Travolta, and "Saturday Night's Alright for Fighting" for *Saturday Night Fever*. Along with everyone else in America that year, I got swept up in the disco craze. I was a freshman at Passaic Valley by then. Heidi had opted for private school in Montclair. A kid named David, the only boy in town who was picked on more than me, took her place in my life. Together, we creamed for Amii Stewart, Alicia Bridges, and Musique's "Push, Push, in the Bush." I wanted to live my life at 120 beats per minute. Strangely, disco—a "lifestyle" movement that had begun in the gay community of New York—marked my last attempt to pass for a girl-chaser in New Jersey.

Flam-
boyant
Like
Me

D i s c o
D o e s n ' t
S u c k

*D*isco officially hus-
tled its way to Little Falls when Passaic Valley's answer
to Sister Sledge—a Russian girl named Satanay, an
Italian *ragazza* named Clementine, and Mary, a Greek
girl whose father owned the Golden Star diner—wore
Gloria Vanderbilt jeans and plastic mules to the freshman awards assembly. For the three years that followed, their legs ended in Candies instead of feet. At
fifteen, I was in awe of them . . . and their plastic
mules.

Footwear had entered my life.

These voluptuous girls, exotic by our standards,
went to New York discos on Saturday nights—all fake
IDs, blow-dried hair, and precocious cleavage. Like
me, they longed for the glamour that the outside world
promised. The difference was that they had boyfriends

old enough to drive, and they got to boogie-oogie-oogie at Studio 54, while I had to make do dancing with myself to Meco's version of the *Close Encounters* theme at the Sunday-afternoon teen disco at the Strawberry Patch in Wayne.

A mirrored ball, dry-ice smoke, and a *Playboy* pinball machine.

Oh, what a hot spot that was.

Every week, after I'd heard Father Gibbons's sermon—he was our "hippie priest," as my mother would say, who walked up and down the aisles while he spoke, treating mass like theater-in-the-round—and then had breakfast at the Versailles Diner in Fairfield, and after that visited Grandpa the loogie-hocker in Paterson, my friend David and I would begin our transformation from Honor Society students into disco studs. At least that's what we thought we looked like once we got dressed. We'd put on our pieced-terry Huk-A-Poo shirts, our indigo Jordache flares with their triple-arc stitching on the back pockets, and the honey-colored Frye boots that we bought on clearance in Paramus, and go dancing. With a home perm that my mother gave me one Saturday afternoon in Nana's dungeon, a full mustache, and tinted glasses, I looked like Jerry the Dentist crossed with Father Guido Sarducci. David, rail-skinny and short, looked like "a snail without a shell." That's what he told me this kid named Kenneth, who was his arch-rival in the reed section of the high school band, always called him.

We weren't pretty, but we felt as cool as Travolta.

A smart kid with more drive than I'd ever have, David wrote poetry, collected stamps, played the clarinet (although not very well), and ate peanut butter on rye and a sleeve of Fudgetown cookies every single day from 1974 to 1980. That is, when he wasn't fending off bullies who made life as big a hell for him as that rotten kid Chooch made mine for me. David and I had first noticed each other when we were nine, seeing in each other's eyes the battle scars of childhood. Although he went to School #3 in Singac and I went to School #1, we had the same catechism class that year. One Sunday morning after we sang "Sons of God"—with its chorus of "*Eat his body! Drink his blood!*"—the teacher, a frowzy woman in a print housedress, read a story about Lazarus. But she kept pronouncing it "La-*zar*-us," which I knew was wrong. She had him mixed up with Lazzara's, which was a baking company in Paterson where my father would get Italian rolls while they were still warm. So I raised my hand and corrected the teacher, who was *not* pleased to have a nine-year-old tell her that she was a nincompoop, although not in so many words. With that, David knew he'd found a kindred spirit.

"You're right," he whispered in a nasal voice. "She's an idiot."

We knew that someday we'd be friends.

Three years later, when we entered junior high, which combined all the seventh- and eighth-graders in town into one throbbing mass of adolescence at School #1, David and I bonded. Ours was a camaraderie of common interests and shared misery. His presence gave me comfort. If nothing else, I knew that as long as he was around, I wasn't the most picked-on person in school. David had that title hands down, getting pushed around, stuffed into his gym locker, and given a wedgie at least once a week. I got threatened, too, and called a fag every single day, but David was called something much worse: Smedley. Chooch named him that. And, everyone, even David's friends, called him "Smeds" before long. He hated that name, but we couldn't help ourselves.

David was *such* a Smedley—painfully underweight, with flat brown hair, wire glasses, and spindly legs always shod in Hush Puppies. He lived in a small white house in Singac, not far from Holy Angels, with his parents, John and Diane, and his little brother, Jim, who was a terror—someone whose idea of fun was to put the family's miniature poodle, Puff, into the dryer and close the door. He couldn't reach the dials, or he surely would have turned it on. He loved torturing his older brother even more. In fact, when he sneaked up behind David and punched him, or doused him with the lawn sprinkler, Jim was almost as gleeful about it as Chooch was.

Everyone liked picking on David, even me sometimes.

We were like partners in crime, though, subversive

in our own geeky way. Holed up on Saturday afternoons in his room, sitting on his twin bed with its Bicentennial-print bedspread, we fancied ourselves a pint-sized Carl Reiner and Mel Brooks, recording *Mad* magazine–style spoofs of movies and TV shows on the Singer cassette recorder my father brought home from work one day. David and I wrote and recorded a cooking show starring Julius Chilled—everything we made was cold—and ad-libbed a morning call-in show named *Little Falls Speaks*, although what it had to say I couldn't tell you. But our masterpiece was a tape-recorded space opera called *Starch Warts*. We wrote it on loose-leaf notebook paper and did all the voices. In our *Star Wars* spoof, Puke Skychucker battled his evil nemesis, Barf Later, with the help of an intergalactic Italian mystic named Bent Cannoli. The script began: "A long time ago, in a galaxy far, far away . . . over a mile and a half, even . . ." and ended when Puke said, "Barf is dead and the universe is safe . . . but this costume is giving me starch warts!" With that, the *Star Wars* theme swelled in the background. In our own private world, we were a laugh riot.

When David and I weren't making tapes for our own amusement, or sitting in the first row to see Woody Allen's *Manhattan* on the day it opened—I could have killed him for picking those seats—we wrote song lists. We'd share a carrel in the quiet section of the library, but instead of writing our papers on *Animal Farm*, we'd take the name of a popular song and suggest who in the news should record it. Number 1, one week, was "I Like Dreamin' " by Karen Ann Quinlan, the comatose woman everyone called New Jersey's favorite vegetable. We had "This Could Be the Start of Something Big" by John Holmes's pediatrician. (I'd seen the well-endowed porn star in a skin magazine.) And, when the ventriloquist Edgar Bergen died, we decided Charlie McCarthy should cover the Rolling Stones song "Miss You." That one made us laugh so hard that Mrs. Ivans yelled at us and asked us to leave if we weren't going to study. But we needed to create such lunacy, Smeds and me.

It was our only escape.

Although David and I took all the advanced placement classes the school offered, we were hardly challenged academically by Passaic Valley. We got straight "A"s without ever really working very hard. The only test of our wills each day was whether we would make it to three o'clock without having food thrown at us whenever we walked through the cafeteria. In the world of movie-parody tapes and song lists that we created, we recast ourselves as funnymen instead of nerds, using humor to stave off teen angst. On tape or on the page, we could be stars, we figured. It was the same on the disco dance floor. There we could shine in a way we never did in gym or after-school sports. There, we could be cool, if not straight.

David liked disco even more than I did. He was mad for Donna Summer. Shortly after "Love to Love

You Baby" hit the charts, he took down all the Stevie Nicks posters in his tiny bedroom and replaced them with images of the disco diva of MacArthur Park. He'd spin her records on an all-in-one phonograph that was cheap, but more high-tech than any high-fidelity piece of equipment any of us owned. It was faux wood-grain and could play anything from 78s to eight-track tapes, which was good because the used Cadillac that my father had just bought had an eight-track tape player in it. So at two in the afternoon, as Frank Senior drove us to the Strawberry Patch, we played David's copy of *Once Upon a Time*.

Checking our parkas when we got there—mine green, David's navy, both with fake fur trim that looked like genuine German shepherd—we'd make our way from the Strawberry Patch's brightly lit foyer, through padded doors with tufted buttons, into the disco darkness. As our eyes adjusted to the simulated night, we'd go to the bar for a Tab, shoehorning our bodies into the throng of kids we didn't know, all waiting to catch the bartender's eye. Then, diet soda in hand, we'd move to the dance floor's fringes, where everyone stood basking in the fractured light radiating off the club's mirrored ball, feet rocking on chunky booted heels.

Strangers to the world of nightclubbery, we talked only to each other, too shy to introduce ourselves to anyone, male or female. No one would dance at the Strawberry Patch, not for a long while anyway. We'd

133

just stand there in our Nik-Nik knockoffs from the Young Men's department at Alexander's, victims of a bad hair age frozen like a magazine layout on seventies glamour don'ts. Not knowing how to flirt, David and I would just look at girls across the lighted dance floor, until something really good like "Native New Yorker" or "Cherchez la Femme" came on. Then the dance floor would get packed, and we would dance alone along the periphery, losing ourselves in the music but making sure no one ever thought we were dancing together. Even if disco had begun as an underground gay phenomenon in New York City, at the Strawberry Patch two boys could not dance together. Not in the afternoon. Not without being called fags, anyway.

When last call came at five-forty-five, we'd clap and beg for one more song. And the DJ would always oblige with "A Fifth of Beethoven" or "I Love the Nightlife," even though it was just getting dark out. Then, as if being dateless weren't bad enough, my father would come into the lobby of the club and yell, "Hey Frankie, come on, let's go." I would die of embarrassment. It was dorky to have your father pick you up, but to have him show his face was even worse. I told my mother what he did and she yelled at him. "Wait in the car, for Christ's sake," she said. "You want him to have a complex?"

Disco, even our afternoon kiddy version, was a link to New York City, and, though I didn't realize it at the time, our first connection to gay culture. It was a tribal drumbeat that lots of not-yet-gay kids heard all over the world. The allure of Studio 54 and Xenon—places I only read about—was that once you got beyond the velvet ropes (no small feat in those days of tyrannical doormen) you got to mix with people who were fabulous. By association, even as far away as Wayne, I felt raised up. Disco didn't suck, as Chooch and a lot of the other kids always said. It was our psychic ticket out of there, a revenge of the nerds set to a thump-thump beat.

As always, TV brought that world home to me. Weeknights at eight-thirty I could watch Grace Jones crawling around in a cage in a leopard catsuit, singing "I Need a Man" on *The Merv Griffin Show.* Sometimes the Village People would be on, too. I loved them, although truth be told, I didn't know they were gay. My cousins—Papa Vic's kids—actually went to see them when they played Madison Square Garden. It was right before the *Live and Sleazy* album came out. My cousins had no idea the Village People were a gay group, either. In any case, they didn't offer to take me along to the concert, and that made me really mad. My mother gave them what-for about it, too, chiding them for not asking their disco-loving younger cousin to go along.

Marian always liked the Village People, especially the blond construction worker, David "Scar" Hodo. She'd say "Oooh, he's so cute, and can he dance!" I would sit there, watching him shake his tool belt on

135

Merv, thinking, "I wonder if he needs a houseboy?" I said this once to my mother, sort of testing the waters with a joke, but she flashed me a look that said, "You'd better be kidding." I didn't make my real feelings about this swivel-hipped construction worker, or *any* construction workers, for that matter, known to her for at least several years.

My disco period was the last time I spent trying to be straight, trying to get Heidi, who'd gone off to private school in junior high, to be my girlfriend. At Montclair Kimberly Academy, mingling with preppies, she'd blossomed into a bodaciously tata-ed beauty, curvaceous in designer jeans and too-tight sweaters. She would have been quite a catch. But in those days, I would have been happy to make *anyone* my girlfriend. I was so lonely and wanted so desperately to prove to my classmates and my parents—if not to myself—that I could be straight, despite mounting evidence to the contrary. The disco seemed a place where I could do that. I was a good dancer. With practice, I figured I could be like John Travolta. He had great clothes and tons of girls. And if he was straight in that white *Saturday Night Fever* suit, I could be, too. But if I was *really* straight, why did I feel such a stirring in my loins during that movie when he sat up in bed, stuck his hand into his black briefs, and fixed himself? That was my favorite moment. My heart nearly leaped out of my chest when he did that. It was so sexy. So provocative.

So fucking Italian.

When *Sarava* went into previews on Broadway, I begged my father to get tickets. *Sarava* was a disco musical based on the movie *Dona Flor and Her Two Husbands* and starred Tovah Feldshuh, whom we knew from *Holocaust* on TV. It was not a high point of Broadway musical history. In fact, it was noteworthy only because there was an original-cast twelve-inch single—a disco remix of the title song—for sale at intermission. I'd never seen that before . . . and haven't since. *Sarava* wasn't *On the Twentieth Century* or *Bent*—or any of the other terrific Broadway shows David and I saw together—but it was disco and that made us happy. As David said during one number, as a burst of synthesizer fireworks filled the theater, "I *love* that sound." We both did.

But only David would attempt to re-create it at home in his living room, on the family organ. He'd begun setting his poetry to a disco beat in hopes that Donna Summer would record one of his songs. He also threw a disco party once when the news said that Skylab was expected to crash back to earth. He lined his garage with Reynolds Wrap and hung Christmas lights from the ceiling. His parents wouldn't allow any liquor at the party, and we were too goody-goody to sneak any in, so we drank C&C cola and danced. That night, we hoped Skylab would crash, right there in Little Falls, preferably *on* David's house. That would've livened things up at least.

Our love of disco and our burgeoning Sunday-afternoon social life led us to the ritual we called disco shopping. I would go to Chess King, usually with David, and, once in a while, with Tommy, who used to live up the street with his widower father, three overweight sisters, two "uncles"—one real, one a "roommate"—and a grandmother who scared all the neighborhood children whenever she went out to sweep the walk. They called her the Witch of Second Avenue, but she was just a tough cookie with a broom, the strength of that cockamamie family. Tommy had moved to Clifton a few years after we met, but we kept in touch. When he left Little Falls, he began life anew, losing weight, becoming popular, and finding a girlfriend. He left a sissy—someone I was sure would be gay, too—and came back macho, with his hair parted in the middle and feathered back with a precision I could only marvel at. Tommy went to a stylist, not a barber like I did, and always carried a plastic rat-tail comb in his back pocket. He kept up with jeans trends like David and I never could, switching from Jordache to Sergio Valente at exactly the right time and leaving us all in the denim dust. Tommy was instrumental in raising my disco awareness. He not only gave me my first pair of designer jeans as a birthday present, but took me to my first concert. It was the Bee Gees live at Madison Square Garden, and they were amazing. We played the *Saturday Night Fever* soundtrack all the way home, and stopped at the

Golden Star for pizza burgers on toasted bagels. We'd each had a beer in the car, so we were a little drunk, too. I felt like a wild man.

Disco shopping with Tommy was an adventure. With him, I discovered footwear that excited me as much as the Candies that Satanay and Clementine and Mary wore. Not content with my Frye boots, I set my sights on a pair of Lucite-heeled lace-ups called Crayons. I saved my money and bought a pair of them in black with red heels right before I graduated high school. I wore them to the senior awards assembly as my favorite disco trio had worn their new Candies three years earlier. I also bought a pair of brown Giorgio Brutini stacked-heel shoes with tennis-ball-yellow piping and laces. They were really pointy and you could see them for blocks. But in case you missed them, I bought socks the exact same optic-yellow color and wore them with the shoes and the jeans that Tommy had given me.

My fashion sense in those days was daring, if nothing else, especially for a compulsive eater like me, whose weight went up and down more often than the New Year's Eve ball in Times Square. My mother would look at me in whatever getup I'd put together —my hair perm-fried; my mustache thicker than Anna DeProspo's—and say in exasperated tones: "You could be *so* attractive if you didn't try so hard to look so ugly." But by then I just figured my style was too sophisticated for her. Only once did my friends have

D i s c o
D o e s n ' t
S u c k

139

the same negative reaction that she did to one of my outfits, and send me back inside to change. That night, during one of my heavy periods, I wore a blue-and-yellow-striped shirt, bright red painter's pants held up with a yellow belt, yellow socks, and those pointy shoes. I looked like a Leo Sayer blowup doll, over-inflated from one too many trips to the anxiety buffet. It was a little much for eating sundaes at the Howard Johnson's over near the A&P. I put on my usual school uniform of a black Elton John concert T-shirt and blue jeans instead. The thumbs-down verdict on my first outfit hurt, but, with a spoon in my mouth, I got past it quickly, overcoming that insult the way I overcame everything else—by eating until I felt better.

A l l
Y o u
C a
E a t

$\mathcal{T}$he sign outside the
old Howard Johnson's, where they served the best
Clam Roll Specials in New Jersey, was missing an
"n," but that only made it better. It said "All You
Ca   Eat" in big black letters against orange, turquoise,
and marquee white. It wasn't as good as the time the
"w" fell off the front of the dinner theater where the
union hall used to be. For weeks, it had said "Conway
T itty" was coming and everyone got a good giggle
as they drove through Little Falls. But "All You
Ca   Eat" was my favorite. I liked the sound of it better than "All You *Can* Eat" because it was more gut-
tural, more primitive, more in keeping with the
voracity with which I sucked up everything that was
not nailed down from the time I was six on.

As Valerie Harper used to say during the opening

monologue of *Rhoda*, "The first thing I remember liking that liked me back was food." For years, it was
my most comforting friend, an unflagging accomplice
in life, something with which I could celebrate my
sun-yellowest highs and escape my blackest lows.
There was nothing that, say, a bowl of pastina with
apple sauce on it—my favorite toddler food—or a
package of Tastykake Butterscotch Krimpets couldn't
cure. And without realizing it, for much of my life I
used food as an answer for everything . . . including
hunger.

Having entered the world a lightweight as a five-
pound-ten-ounce "tumor," I was not destined to be
fat. But when I was in the first grade, I had my tonsils
out, and I became a power eater almost overnight.
"You started eating then and you haven't stopped
since," my mother said to me when I was in my teens.
And, she was absolutely right, if a tad indelicate. Years
later, when I bought a paperback copy of *The James
Coco Diet* at a tag sale in East Hampton, I read that
he too had been a skinny kid who became a butterball
after his tonsillectomy. The late actor, who played
funny gay neighbors better than anyone, learned as a
child in the hospital that he could put pain on hold
and keep fear at bay if he gorged himself on gallons
of ice cream. He was done in, for much of his life, by
Butter Brickle and well-meaning parents. But then,
who wasn't?

If you were having a problem—say you were gay

and kids picked on you unmercifully—you could find solace at our house in an inexhaustible supply of white boxes with midnight-blue lettering. We were an Entenmann's family. At any given time, there would be open boxes of Crumb Coffee Cake, Blueberry Beehive Pie, Fudge Brownies, and Sour Cream Pound Cake. We used to buy them in bulk at the Entenmann's outlet, which was a hub of local activity and one of Little Falls' most attractive features. We'd never miss a yellow-line/three-for-a-dollar sale. On those days, Italian women in black hairnets and hot-pink stretch pants would wrestle each other for Apple Puffs that had too much icing on them, but were still good. At our house, we didn't mind such sticky imperfections because we figured that you could always hide them with a scoop of Welsh Farms ice cream. A half gallon of Coffee Royale was always in the freezer. It was Merv Griffin's favorite flavor. That's what my father said, anyway. He'd heard it someplace and that sold him on it. For some reason, my father's devotion to Merv was unswerving.

As if ice cream and Entenmann's were not enough, there were always open packages of Vienna Fingers in the cabinet under the counter, half-full cans of Pringle's potato chips in the bread box, and, once in a while, if Marian was feeling festive, Snack Mate spray cheese in a can to put on Triscuits. On birthdays and holidays, the number of junk food offerings would multiply with Duncan Hines cake-mix cakes swathed

A l l
Y o u
C a
E a t

143

in Ready-to-Spread frosting. Food coloring made them even more special. We had a bright yellow smiley-face cake one birthday; a red-white-and-blue Bicentennial cake in 1976; and a cake shaped like a bunny and covered with Angel Flake coconut one Easter from a recipe straight out of *Woman's Day*. One February, we baked a heart-shaped layer cake with pink icing and used red Write-A-Cake to spell out "Love Will Keep Us Together." That was at the height of the Captain and Tennille's popularity. It was just one more reason to believe that *everything* could be translated into food if you had a mind for it. And, on Prospect, we did.

Although my mother was not a particularly good cook—"instant" was her favorite kitchen word—she believed in food and reveled in the pleasures of consumption. From her, I learned that you could give up cake for Lent and still eat hot cross buns (because, technically, they were bread), and that a home is not a home without a springform pan and a cheesecake to put in it. She ate slowly and persistently, savoring every morsel as if it were her last, delighting each night in guilt-inducing desserts washed down with Tetley, the tiny little tea leaf tea, while the TV blared away on the porch.

Although he always had ulcers and sipped Mylanta like after-work martinis, my father didn't believe in skimping when it came to food, either. Saturday night, he'd cook and we'd always eat steak and french fries and an iceberg salad with Pathmark French dressing, which was a very 1960s shade of bright orange. On Sundays, while plate spinners spun plates on sticks and Topo Gigio did his thing on *The Ed Sullivan Show*, my father would grill American cheese on Wonder Bread and make his usual Pop Art Pathmark salad. When he was really famished, he'd say, "I could eat the ass out of a possum, I'm so hungry." On those nights, even though it was just the three of us (four if we sent some down to Nana), he'd pick up a square pizza from Sun-Ray Pizzeria that was so big it came in two boxes. Twenty-four pieces, gobbed with cheese; the best in the neighborhood and all for us.

"You eat good, you shit good," my father'd always say.

Non-Italians, or what I like to call white people, would marvel at the exalted place eating occupied in our lives. Our neighbors Jack and Vivian, for instance, were agog the first time they came for dinner. They didn't know that a huge plate of Celentano frozen manicotti meant that a roast chicken—and not dessert—was on deck. The Entenmann's, they didn't realize, came much later . . . with espresso and a shot of anisette, if my parents were really pulling out all the stops. The pasta course was just to whet your appetite, a starchy little two-thousand-calorie starter.

Eating would not have been a problem had I not been warped in my earliest years by instructions that defied all logic and taught me to ignore any internal hunger cues . . . if I'd ever waited long enough to *have*

A l l
Y o u
C a
E a t

145

a hunger pang, which I rarely did. The notion of portion control went right out the window, thanks to Marian and Frank Senior. They would say, when I was the tiniest child, "If you're full, just eat the meat, don't eat the bread." They never once said, "If you're full, stop eating." Why stop at full when you could go on to big-as-a-house, bust-a-gut bloated? My grandmother didn't help matters any, either. When she baby-sat me, she'd feed me an entire can of Niblets corn, which was about my favorite food.

I'm sure my family's penchant for stuffing my little mouth had something to do with living through the Depression, though it could just have been that they were Italian and crazy. But that was the kind of stuff they taught. That, and never make chicken salad out of fresh chicken. If it was fresh, you should eat it plain. If it was old and just about to turn—well, *that's* when it was okay to mask it with mayonnaise and make chicken salad.

Sometimes I wonder how I got out of my childhood alive.

Growing up in that house, I developed what I like to call my single-serving theory, which I spent many years researching. I believed that any package you opened—regardless of what it said on the label—was a single serving, no matter how big it was. If you opened a pint of ice cream, it was meant to be eaten in its entirety. A quart wasn't meant for two people, it was just a bigger challenge for one, namely me. Funny Bones came two to a pack, but you were obviously supposed to eat them both. Because if you were supposed to stop at one, they'd wrap them individually, right? The Oreo people understood this better than anyone, packaging their cookies in two different ways. If you were a big eater, or particularly distraught over, say, getting a C in gym, you could buy Oreos in a cello-wrapped package with three rows of cookies. But if you only wanted a few cookies, say fifteen or twenty, you could buy them in the cardboard box with three stay-fresh plastic sleeves inside. Then, you'd only have to eat one whole row instead of three.

This made perfect sense to me and was an integral part of what I call the salt/sweet cycle, which I practiced regularly. This was the eating spiral by which a craving for something salty, once satisfied, leads to a longing for something sweet, which, in turn, leads to a desire for something salty, then something sweet, then salty, then sweet, and so on and so forth. This continued until you were so nauseated, you no longer remembered that you were depressed. For years, I believed that salted peanuts mixed with plain M&M's were nature's most perfect food. Trail mix for food abusers, it was the salt/sweet cycle with one-bowl convenience. Genius.

My epitaph will read: "He Was a Good Eater." Because eating *is* what I'm best at. But as a kid, I wrapped my overeating in a cloak of self-deprecation. After being a target for too many years, I developed the classic first-strike mentality, making jokes at my own expense so as to beat the other kids to the punch. This is a way to keep some power in a situation over which you have little control. At school, I would joke about doing a cannonball into our backyard swimming pool and displacing an amount of water equal to a Buick. All the kids got a big laugh out of that, and I yucked it up along with them—and then went back to eating and being miserable. I didn't want to be fat, but it seemed to suit me, like squishy pink armor telling the world to stay away. I was safeguarded in my solitude, but dismal in my own skin, of which there always seemed to be too much.

My mother didn't help matters. She believed my weight problem would be outgrown, and all I needed to do, until that glorious day when we left the Sears Husky Boys Department for good, was wear my shirts untucked and pulled down as far over my butt as possible. This camouflaging practice works about as well as comb-over hairdos that part just above the ear to hide baldness. But she would tug at my clothes as I left for school, say, "Keep your shirt down in the back," and pretend that that made everything all better.

It didn't.

Although I was a husky and not a huge, I felt so

unattractive, so misshapen, so uncomfortable in my own body, that I believed I was unworthy of any kind of love or affection. I took these feelings with me into adulthood, playing the role of fat and funny—a homo- with no -sexual to speak of. I would lose weight periodically, thirty pounds at a clip. Start looking really good, meet a boy, fall in love, go out for a while, break up, gain it all back again, and go into hiding. In the gay male world, if you want to disappear, just gain weight. You no longer come up on gaydar. You can pass through life undetected, like a pudgy Romulan Bird of Prey with a cloaking device on maximum. It was a vicious circle, this weight roller coaster. And I would ride it periodically, throughout my life. I still do. You never really get off it. If you're lucky, and I was, the hills just get smaller, the gains and losses less steep. Your self-esteem reaches a high enough level that you don't have to sabotage yourself completely every time you meet with some disappointment in your life.

It is a hard role to shake, though—this funny-fat thing. Even when you begin liking the person you see staring back at you in the mirror, you remember the hurt: All those times you were picked last in gym. The afternoon when you sat in the dentist's office across from your high school and your classmate, the part-time hygienist, didn't know the waiting room window was open and shouted to her friend outside, "Guess who have I to go work on now? Frank DeCaro! Ewwww!" But you have to shake it.

Now, as an adult, I sometimes think life is like that episode of *The Mary Tyler Moore Show* where Rhoda goes to Calorie Cutters and loses twenty pounds. Her colleagues at the department store where she works in display enter her in the Miss Hempel's beauty contest. She says she's just there to make the other girls look good. But she musters her courage and goes through with it. The night of the contest, she comes home looking great in a black halter dress with her hair all up, seventies style, to tell Mary and their neighbor Phyllis Lindstrom that it wasn't a total disaster. She didn't win, she came in third. When Phyllis leaves, though, Rhoda confides in Mary that she didn't come in third. She actually won. She goes out into the hall, puts on a faux-ermine-trimmed cape, a Miss Hempel's sash, and a crown from the junk jewelry department, and grabs her rhinestone-encrusted scepter. Phyllis, of course, returns to see Rhoda in her regalia. "Boy, they sure make a fuss over third place," Phyllis says. Rhoda turns, after all those years of being the fat funny girl, and snaps "*I won, Cookie.*"

By the time I was in my junior year in high school, I was itching to win, too. I'd been on a serious diet, and for once I had stuck to it. I was thinner than I'd ever been. With that, came the beginnings of confidence. During the months that followed, I decided theater was going to be my life. That was when I met a kid who wasn't like any other boy I'd ever met. His name was Kenneth; he sat in front of David in band and always called him a slug. As my life changed and Kenneth and I became friends, I realized it wouldn't be long before I had to tell Smedley good-bye.

He *didn't* take it well.

B y e
B y e
S m e d l e y

*T*here had never been
much appreciation for art in our house—unless you
counted macramé owls and paint-by-number clowns
—but Broadway, well, that was always tops in taps
with my mother. Lee J. Cobb in *Death of a Salesman*,
Ethel Merman in *Gypsy*, Sammy Davis, Jr., in *Mr.
Wonderful*—Marian had seen them all. She would tell
stories about sitting next to Angela Lansbury at *The
Boy Friend* with Julie Andrews, getting Hopalong Cassidy's autograph and nearly fainting because he was the
most handsome man she'd ever seen, and being stared
at by Milton Berle, who, she says, got mad because
she didn't make a fuss over him.

"Who knew it was him?" she'd say.

As a kid, I'd eat these stories up like so much popcorn at an after-school double feature. It was like being

let in on a former life, a life in which I imagined my mother a film noir–ish femme fatale—veiled hat, slim skirt, nails the color of claret—surrounded by handsome men in broad-shouldered suits and wearing fedoras. As pasts go, Marian's was pretty glamorous, especially for someone I knew best in a housedress and slipper-socks, cooking a turkey roast on 350 degrees, and waiting for *Jeopardy* to start. As a teenager, I wanted her present life to be glamorous, too. When we started going to the theater together, it was. Well, sort of, anyway.

Once each season, Marian's girlfriend Rose's husband, Jimmy, the electrician, would buy four tickets to whatever show the Montclair Operetta Club was putting on and give them to his wife to use. In our neighborhood, husbands didn't go to the theater unless it was a school production and their kids were performing. The Montclair Operetta Club's shows were always big musicals on shoestring budgets—*The King and I* with a skin wig—and my father's high school classmate Norm, who was what they called a confirmed bachelor back in those days, would act in them. Next to our pastor, who looked like Peter Finch and had a brogue to die for, Norm treated me with more respect as a child than anyone else. Whenever we met after mass on the steps of Holy Angels, he wouldn't ask me stupid questions like "You got a girlfriend yet?" or attempt to shadow-box with me, like my father's other friends would. Instead, he'd ask me about whatever grammar school play I was in, and tell me about his own experiences in community theater. To me, Norm was a celebrity, the Little Falls equivalent of Monty Woolley, and I liked him a lot. He was practically famous, and at six feet tall, with reddish-brown hair, fair skin, and a bushy mustache, he was decidedly more handsome than most men I knew.

Anyway, Marian and her friend Rose and *her* friend Rose, who smoked and sounded like Selma Diamond, and I would pile into the first Rose's Cadillac and go see *1776* or *The Music Man* or whatever they were doing. If the show was good, and sometimes it was, we stayed for the whole thing and then went out for coffee-and. But if it wasn't, like the season they did *Song of Norway*, my mother would say at intermission, "Do you want to stay until the end or should we go get pancakes?" And invariably, before the entr'acte was finished, we'd be on our way to Perkin's Pancake House. There we'd eat pigs in a blanket while smoky Rose inhaled Virginia Slims and left lipstick smudges on a cracked but bottomless cup of Joe.

Sitting in a booth, Marian and me on one side, the two Roses on the other, I'd listen as they gossiped about our across-the-street neighbor who tried to off herself every six months and about the Puerto Rican family that moved in down the block much to the consternation of everyone's parents on Prospect Street. "If Consuelo over there thinks I'm going to let her kids use my pool, she can go scratch," Rose would say.

The other Rose would take a drag on her cigarette, and then in Gravel Gertie's voice say, "Frig her."

It was a very big deal to me, these once-a-season standing dates with three menopausal Italian women. Although I was only thirteen or fourteen, on my nights out with the girls I got to be a grown-up, and I fit right in. After all, they liked what I liked—food, shopping, men, and, of course, the theater—so there was never a lull in the conversation. Because of these women, I became a theater groupie, forcing my parents to buy *The New York Times* every Sunday so I could devour the "Arts & Leisure" section and keep up with everything that was going on (and going up) on the Great White Way. The more I read, the more I longed to go to New York.

When I turned fifteen, my father brought home two tickets—one for Mom, one for me; God forbid he should go with us—to my first Broadway musical. It was *The Magic Show* starring that rabbit-faced magician Doug Henning and written by Stephen Schwartz, the guy who wrote *Godspell.* It was a dinner-and-theater package, which included a bus from the plant where my father worked and back. As it turned out, Henning had already left the show by the time those of us in the Kearfott group got there. His replacement was not quite a star of the same magnitude. In fact, the guy's name was misspelled in the *Playbill* and they had to stick in a piece of paper with the right spelling. How embarrassing for him . . . and for me.

I mean, as beginnings go, this wasn't Ethel Merman in *Gypsy*. But that night, up in the cheap seats with Marian, the femme fatale, at my elbow, during a song called "Solid Silver Platform Shoes," a show-tune queen was born.

We saw a lot of great stuff, my mother and me. There was *Dracula* with a totally hot Frank Langella and those wonderful Edward Gorey sets; *Ain't Misbehavin'* with Nell Carter, all jelly and shake; and *A Chorus Line*, which spoke to every gay kid who saw it, to none more than me. Oh, I may not have been out of the closet that night on Shubert Alley, but I knew what I was seeing in *A Chorus Line*—myself. I identified with the gay characters, their need to escape unhappy home lives and follow their dreams. "Kiss today good-bye and point me toward tomorrow"— that's how I felt in Little Falls. I howled, more than I should have, I guess, when one said something like "I thought about committing suicide, but in Buffalo, suicide is redundant." Yes! I thought.

These shows and these early trips into Manhattan, with their package-deal dinners, gave me a taste of the life I longed to lead. From the moment I saw New York City at night, my face pressed to the windows of that chartered bus, I knew this was where I wanted to be. Here was excitement and energy instead of the stultifying sameness of suburbia. In the city, there was the comfort of anonymity. No one there knew how often the other kids called me a fag, or spat on me,

B y e
B y e
s m e d l e y

157

or tried to stuff me in a locker. The city that my father called a jungle and TV commercials called Fun City was a place where I knew I would feel at home, where I knew there'd be lots of other people like me, even if I didn't know exactly who I was yet. And, it couldn't be any more dangerous than walking through the Passaic Valley High School cafeteria, no matter what my father said.

That was where I feared for my life, not on Forty-sixth Street.

Back at Passaic Valley, theater proved my salvation. In theater I could be part of a team that, unlike Little League and all those skins-versus-shirts kickball games, I actually wanted to be on. During my junior year, I began hanging around with the Masque & Sandal troupe, which was basically any kid in the class who was willing to stay after school, learn lines, and get up in front of the rest of the high school for two nights in the fall and two in the spring. You didn't have to be that good an actor, just nervy. We did have a star that year, a girl named Donna Marie Elio who ended up in the original Broadway cast of Stephen Sondheim's *Merrily We Roll Along*. She was a huge encouragement to me, suggesting I audition for the senior class musical, and she fed my dreams of becoming an actor. As a little girl, she'd toured in *Gypsy* with Angela Lansbury, so if she said I had *something,* I figured she was right. What I really wanted, though, wasn't to be an actor, but to be famous enough to be on talk shows.

Not the tabloidy kind they have today, but shows like *The Mike Douglas Show* and *Merv*. I've always wanted to sit between Kaye Ballard and Hermione Gingold and chat with Charles Nelson Reilly about playing Hoo Doo on *Lidsville*.

That was my real dream.

Anyway, when I first began going to Masque & Sandal meetings in the school auditorium, they were rehearsing *Grease*. I arrived too late to do anything but watch, but that was okay. Mr. DePascuale had given the part of Danny Zuko to a pimply-faced, gangly nerd who was near the top of his class and not even Italian. I liked that. I figured if *he* could get a role meant for John Travolta, I could get a good part, too, in next year's musical, which was to be *Bye Bye Birdie*.

But all was not bliss. The one thing that said the most to me about life at Passaic Valley—even in the drama club—was that the teacher let the girl playing Rizzo in *Grease* change one of the lines. In "Summer Nights," when she was supposed to say " 'Cause he sounds like a drag," she said "like a fag" instead. Everyone thought that was hilarious, especially accompanied by a big limp-wrist gesture. The teacher did nothing. I always resented him for that, just like I resented every other teacher who did nothing to protect would-be gay kids from their tormentors.

But even with its share of homophobia, the drama club offered an atmosphere in which I could come out of my shell, if not come out of the closet. The acting

I'd done behind the closed door of David's bedroom-cum-recording-studio whetted my appetite for the stage. The chance to actually make an audience laugh was irresistible to me, now that I'd found some confidence and a waist size that wasn't ridiculously large for a five-foot-eight-inch sixteen-year-old.

When it came time to audition for *Birdie* in the spring of 1979, the teacher asked us to get up onstage in the auditorium and introduce ourselves and then just talk for a few minutes. I wanted the part of the father, Harry MacAfee, more than anything, because Paul Lynde, whom I'd always idolized, played him on Broadway. Like a lot of gay boys, I had been doing a drop-dead Paul Lynde impression since I'd first seen him as Uncle Arthur on *Bewitched* and Dr. Dudley on *The Munsters*. "That's disgusting" was my catch-all catch-phrase for years. I waited nervously in my seat as each boy and girl got up and introduced themselves and talked about why they wanted to be in the senior class musical. When it came time for my turn, I edged my way out of my row about a quarter of the way back in the auditorium, trotted down the aisle, and bounded up the stairs to the stage. Turning to face my classmates and the teacher, I introduced myself, standing there in a black-and-white-striped terrycloth shirt and white canvas jeans. I wanted to play Harry MacAfee, I said, because I loved Paul Lynde.

"Actually, I, uh, *do* Paul Lynde," I said.

"Then do him for us," Mr. DePascuale said.

And, with only a moment's hesitation, I launched into a TV commercial that Paul had been doing for a New York bank. I knew the spot cold. "Open up, open up, I know it isn't nine o'clock yet, but some of us have to go to work," I said, shaking my head, wrinkling my nose, and stretching the word "work" into several syllables just like he would. I did the whole thirty-second commercial, ending with "You're all being very nice . . . and I don't like it." But when the kids applauded my audition piece, I *did* like it. After years of torment, they were actually applauding me. I couldn't believe it. I was practically shaking, my hands were like ice, but I was exhilarated. For the first time in my school life, I didn't feel like the class pariah. The applause was my first glimpse of acceptance by my peers. And, best of all, it had nothing to do with my being a good student. Instead, they liked me because I was funny and outgoing and brave enough to get up before them. They made me feel popular. Popularity was what I, like every teenager, wanted most. At dinner that night, as I poured ketchup on my mother's signature overcooked meatloaf, I told my parents how well my audition had gone.

"Oh, honey, I hope you get the part," Marian said.

"Yeah," my father added without much conviction, "me, too."

A few days later, when the cast list was posted near the auditorium after school, I nervously approached the bulletin board, looking for my name next to

Harry's, not knowing quite what I'd do if it wasn't. Thank heaven, that's exactly where my name was written. I'd gotten the Paul Lynde part. I couldn't wait for senior year to begin so we could actually start rehearsing.

When the new term did finally begin, the first week in September, we practiced for hours every day after school in the auditorium, while other kids built and painted sets and ordered a gold lamé Elvis jumpsuit from a rental house for Ricky, the guy who was playing Birdie, to wear. I borrowed clothes from my father for me, talked my mother into lending us some shirtwaist dresses for Kim, the girl playing Mrs. MacAfee, and bought the original cast album so I could practice singing "Hymn for a Sunday Evening (Ed Sullivan)" and "Kids"—my two songs—at home.

I wasn't much of a singer, but neither was Paul.

During rehearsal, those of us who were principals in the cast became good friends. We spent so much time with each other, we didn't have time for anyone else. On Fridays, happy with our work and the new friendships we were forging, we'd go to Howard Johnson's to celebrate. When they brought our Fudgana sundaes—which I always pronounced "Fud-ghana" because there was no "e"—we'd break into "The Telephone Hour" in full voice, until the manager threatened to kick·us out.

The fun I had had with David paled in comparison with the raucousness I shared with these kids. My interest in him was diminishing rapidly, and he was none too pleased. I wasn't very good at hiding the fact that I liked my new friends better—especially one boy I'd met junior year, not in Masque & Sandal, but in coordinate geometry. Kenneth was introverted and a good-looking boy, and hated David only as much as David hated him. Kenneth was the guy who said Smedley looked like a snail without a shell. His arch-rival.

I thought he was the cutest boy at Passaic Valley.

When it came time for the show, we sold out our two performances. After all that effort, that's all there were. Tickets cost $3; too little, we thought. On opening night, October 19, 1979, Marian brought Nana, Rose, Vera, and my father, who for once was excited to see his son excelling at something other than school-work. From the overture to the curtain call, it was a blur for me. The performance went off pretty much without a hitch, except when I said, "I've got one thing to say," and someone sneezed so loudly back-stage that everyone looked away. I had to get focus back, so I ad-libbed "That's not it!" with a big Paul Lynde–as–Hollywood Square flourish, and everyone laughed. My big moment, though, came during the "Ed Sullivan" number. Harry MacAfee, delirious that he is to appear on that show, says mid-song: "I've got a wonderful wife, two swell kids, a good job and now this . . ." and then laughs in that throaty snicker of his. They rolled in the aisles at Passaic Valley with that—and when the show was over and I took my bow, I could hear Marian yelling her head off and applauding like crazy. I loved every minute of the adoration, especially from my father.

"Hey, buddy, you were terrific," he said in the dressing room afterwards.

The next day, there were congratulatory phone calls galore, and Michele—the other girl, besides Heidi, whom I dated in high school—stopped by our house with half a dozen long-stemmed red roses. I couldn't wait to do the show again that night. Backstage afterwards, one of the guidance counselors sent me a note saying that her husband rarely laughed, but he did at my antics in *Bye Bye Birdie* the night before and she wanted to say thanks. I was in heaven, not only because the show had gone well on opening night and closing night the day after, but because I was now part of the in crowd. From the cast party on, I was strictly A-list at Passaic Valley.

For the first time in my life, I got invited to good parties—parties other kids talked about the following week, not to make fun of, as they'd done with David's tinfoil Skylab party. Instead, I was going to real parties, noisy ones with liquor, held when kids' parents weren't home. The best was the one at Sara Jane's house, when we all got drunk on Boone's Farm Apple Wine and played Devo's *Are We Not Men?* album on her little brother's Close-'N'-Play phonograph. David would *never* have been invited to such a thing.

I learned to air-kiss with this new crowd of theater

kids. And what I kissed most was my old friends good-bye. I no longer wanted to be part of a friendship that, like mine with David, was based on mutual unhappiness. I wanted to be associated with cool kids, ones who had girlfriends or boyfriends, fashionable clothes, cars of their own; kids who weren't picked on their entire life for being different. Smedley, with whom I'd shared my misfit sorrows for so many years, didn't take well to my newfound popularity and the distance I was consciously putting between the two of us. In my yearbook, he wrote: " 'Bye Bye Birdie.' Your acting was good in it. Afterward, your personality changed. Kissing girls in the hallway, saying you cared about everyone and loved everyone who walked by—your acting was even better then. Instant fame! You were finally in the 'in' group. It was what you wanted."

He was right. I was guilty as charged, but I wasn't looking back. I knew I couldn't take him with me. David was still Smedley in everyone's eyes, still someone who got called a fag every single day. I, on the other hand, had become a star at Passaic Valley, and no one called me names anymore. Thanks to *Bye Bye Birdie*, I said hello to a brand-new life. What irked David more than anything was that I had become good friends with Kenneth. He would have died if he'd known his arch-rival and I began dating each other right after *Bye Bye Birdie* closed.

That "Ghoul"

$\mathcal{N}$o one took coordinate geometry to find a boyfriend—except, of course, for Petey's trampy sister Roxanne, who moved into the math teacher's one-bedroom apartment somewhere near Succasunna shortly after she graduated. We took the class because the teacher was a dude and everyone knew it. A pocky James Woods type, the guy was a leftover hippie who was so dazed and confused some days that he couldn't do the proofs that he'd start on the blackboard. He'd try one theorem and then another and then get lost and say, "Oh, fuck this," and dismiss class early. We liked him a lot—so much, in fact, that parents began to get suspicious. Once we got called before the board of education because someone had suggested that the teacher was Little Falls' answer to Jim Jones and that before long all his students would be drinking tainted Kool-Aid with our official Hornet-burgers in the Passaic Valley cafeteria, but it never happened.

Anyway, it was in this hotbed of mathematical theory that I met Kenneth, David's sworn enemy and my first hunk of burning love, folded pretzel-style into a too-small school desk in the front row near the windows. He was doing mental calisthenics and looking just too fabulous. Well, he looked fabulous for that time, anyway. He was tall, seventies skinny—with no chest to speak of and slightly wide, almost girly hips that made him look like David Bowie in *The Elephant Man*. He was lanky, with dirty-blond hair that fell in his eyes—except for that awful time he went to Hair Say and got a body wave. And he had the most beautiful hands I'd ever seen in my life.

His were not the hands of someone who retrieved shopping carts from the parking lot of ShopRite, although that's what he did after school. They were the hands of an intellectual, with long, tanned fingers that looked best curled around a Marlboro and a ratty paperback copy of some Sartre or other, with nervous nails he'd rub together until they were worn down like beach glass. They looked like the gold-leaf praying-Jesus hands on my mother's smoked-glass, pride-and-joy coffee table, the one with the gold legs with faux gemstones that matched her purple couch. Kenneth later said he thought they looked like E.T.'s phone home fingers, and maybe they did. But at the time I loved them—mostly because they were attached to him, which I soon became, too.

Although Kenneth was really just a bookish kid with a beanbag chair and a thing for German Expressionist film—and not the cause-less rebel that I romantically imagined him to be—he *was* the boy I'd been looking for, the soul mate who shared my desire for escape and the will to really make it happen. Marian and Frank had taught me what was good. Ken—bless his heart—arrived in time to teach me what was bad. In him, I found someone who would stay up late and think existential thoughts, hang out at the Versailles diner drinking coffee and munching *sfogliatelle* until the wee hours, and go to midnight showings of *The Rocky Horror Picture Show* at the Rockaway Town Square mall dressed like a Transylvanian freak. Finally, *someone* was there to teach the goody-goody nerd I had become what all the drug paraphernalia at Smuggler's Attic—our local black-lit head shop—was used for, even if I never had any intention of actually using any of it.

To me, Kenneth was beautiful and dangerous, angst personified. A tall, big-toothed boy from the other side of the tracks—West Paterson—who was born to wear Levi 501s and ran with a rough crowd. Well, one rougher than I did, anyway. Until Kenneth arrived, my circle of friends consisted of Smedley, several members of the literary magazine staff, and a kinky-haired Italian girl I had a crush on, whom everyone called Sasquatch. Neither she, nor the situation, was pretty.

Kenneth, however, was something else.

He didn't stay home and make tapes or go to the Strawberry Patch on Sunday afternoons. Kenneth didn't get his kicks playing with a Cuisinart like I did, either. (I was the only boy—and, I'd venture to say, the only person of any age or gender—at Passaic Valley High School to own his own food processor in 1979. I'd gotten it from my mother for my birthday, after a year of visiting it at Bamberger's housewares department, much to my father's dismay. Not only had his son flunked Little League, but now he was spending his after-school hours julienning! Frank Senior was not happy.)

Kenneth smoked dope, drank Jack Daniel's, listened to Patti Smith on WNEW, and hung out with girls with nicknames like Zala-chops who'd steal beakers full of compounds from the chem lab and throw them out the window like lethal water balloons. He wore vintage clothes and plaid flannel shirts with the sleeves cut off and concert T-shirts for bands that would surely have given my father a second heart attack if he'd ever stopped and paid attention to their lyrics. Basically, Kenneth was "grunge" before grunge was Grunge—sort of a low-rent River Phoenix years before his time.

If Kenneth wasn't my knight in plaid flannel, he was someone to take me away from the teacher's-pet persona I'd cultivated so successfully. The two of us were an odd couple, to be sure—a willowy blond and a thinner-but-still-doughy brunet, we looked like the number 18 whenever we stood next to each other. But somehow it worked. Our opposites attracted. Kenneth was punk. I was disco. He was Neil Young in Rod Stewart's body. I was Bette Midler in Elton John's. We were perfect for each other . . . or so I thought at sixteen and seventeen.

On our first date—although neither of us knew it was a date—we went to Willowbrook, a mall that shares its name with a mental hospital, and not without reason. His mother drove us, because we only had our learner's permits. After shopping Harmony Hut and Chess King, we ate gyros sitting on the floor of the mall, with that goopy white sauce rolling down our arms. It was so romantic, and so unlike the other 9,467 visits I'd made to that mall since it opened in 1969. After lunch, already dreaming dreams of blissful domesticity, I asked Kenneth if he'd come up to the linens department at Stern's to look at sheets with me.

"They're having a white sale," I told him. "I *love* white sales."

"You love *white sales?*" Kenneth asked incredulously.

He'd never met anyone who got worked up over terms like "200-thread-count" and "percale" before. To him, sheets were sheets. To me, they were the future, a stylish step toward my own apartment far away from Little Falls. I'd wanted to move out since I was four or five. My original plan, concocted in about the first grade, was to move into the space under one of the shirt counters at the Great Eastern Mills, a big barn of a bargain store where Nana had worked. I used to love to play in those spaces, imagining how I would decorate the place. It would be small but cute, I figured, and to furnish it, I would need miniature appliances. So I asked my parents for—and got—a Suzy Homemaker washer. Wise to my plan and, I think, worried I might grow up to be a sissy, they drew the line at an E-Z Bake Oven.

"F. A. I.," my father said when I asked for one. "Forget About It."

That spring, I got to know Kenneth's family—his sister, Barbara, who looked like Toni Tennille, his mother, Eleanor, who from day one plied me with pastry then called me a "gigunda" for eating too much, and his quiet father, Tony, who was a dead ringer for Barney Hefner, Archie Bunker's pal on *All in the Family*. Kenneth's mother could perk coffee better than anyone, and played a good round of golf, but she was also the most self-centered woman ever to pick up a percolator or a set of clubs. She was not what you'd call warm, especially not to Kenneth.

Eleanor always called him a ghoul because he liked to stay up late with his stereo headphones on, or hanging on the telephone talking to me. Worse yet, she once told Kenneth that he was an unwanted child, and

I dare say both she and he believed it. Tony didn't help matters. He dealt with his wife by zoning out and, like so many fathers of his generation, didn't pay attention to anything or anyone, not even his son, who needed him most.

No wonder Kenneth did drugs.

It wasn't long before Eleanor asked me to go with them on vacation. I was a personable kid, with good manners around adults, and she figured I'd keep her son out of trouble. (If she'd only known.) Kenneth's parents were campers who owned a big Winnebago that they'd pull to one of the New Jersey beaches and live out of for a week at a time. I'd never done this sort of thing before. My family always stayed in motels—Marian loved the Internationale on the beach in Wildwood Crest. For a vacation breakfast, we wouldn't dream of building a fire. Instead, we'd eat Entenmann's and drink Sanka in Cozy Cups; then we'd send my father out for scrambled-egg sandwiches on white toast with ketchup and salt and pepper. It was like having room service and being related to the waiter.

Despite my non-outdoorsy nature, I jumped at the chance to go camping. I'd have done *anything* to be with Kenneth. Without realizing it, during the summer of 1979, between my junior and senior years in high school, I was falling in love. One morning at the beach, before anyone was awake, I woke up and just began to stare at Kenneth, trying to drink him in like so much Fresca. I'd only been staring for twenty or thirty minutes when he woke up suddenly and caught me.

"What are you looking at?" he said.

"Nothing," I replied. "Just you."

It sounded weird, and it was. I didn't quite understand my fascination with him. It wasn't anything I'd ever felt before. I mean, I wasn't lying there thinking of 101 Ways to Share a Sleeping Bag, but there *was* something going on that I couldn't quite come to grips with. It was big love. It was big lust.

Hell, it was just *big*.

During our nightly phone conversations, Kenneth and I had danced around the topic of homosexuality without ever addressing it directly. We'd broached bisexuality, which was an easier topic. It always is, until you finally come out and are living your life as an openly gay man, at which point it becomes something for which you have no patience. (Bisexuals, I've come to realize as an adult, are troublesome because they can leave you for twice as many people.) One night, though, I told Kenneth that I thought I was attracted to both men and women. Ever the math student, he asked for percentages. I'm sure I said "Fifty–fifty." Kenneth, bolder than I, said he thought he was more 70–30, with a marked preference for men. Ultimately, we both decided it was 90–10 for me and 100 percent for Mr. Kinsey 6. But at the time, we were relieved to be bisexual instead of gay or straight. The following morning, I awoke feeling more relieved and energetic and happy than I'd ever felt in my entire life. I felt that morning like I'd joined a country club.

And, in a way, I had.

The week before my seventeenth birthday, which was the month after *Bye Bye Birdie* closed, we were in Kenneth's bedroom one night, sitting on his bed, with the FM radio bouncing off the knotty-pine paneling, and I felt one of his magnificent coffee-table-Jesus hands take mine. Soon we were in each other's arms, our hearts racing, first with fear, then with abandon. We kissed, his tongue parting my lips. Kenneth's kisses were nothing like Michele's or Heidi's. These were man kisses. How strange his teenaged whiskers felt upon my face. So new, yet oddly familiar. We necked for an hour; afraid of what we'd started, we never let our hands stray past each other's chest. Then Eleanor shouted up the stairs that it was getting late. I had to go. In silence, Kenneth drove me home, our hands intertwined on the luggage-brown seats of his father's white Ford Fairmont.

"I'll see you at school tomorrow," he said, his hand pulling away from mine, as he made the turn into our driveway on Prospect.

"Tomorrow *night,* too?" I asked.

"Yeah," he said through the open car window. "After dinner."

My father was already asleep when I got home that night; my mother, as usual, was reading the newspaper

A
B o y
N a m e d
P h y l l i s

in her BarcaLounger and watching TV at the same time. I said the quickest hello-and-good-night in history, gave her a peck on the cheek, and slipped down the hall to my room. Closing the door as quietly as I could, clicking the button lock with the knob turned so it wouldn't make any noise, I stripped, jumped in bed, and within seconds had the orgasm I'd been waiting almost seventeen years to have.

I ejaculated so much I thought I was going to drown.

The next day, Kenneth and I kept our distance from each other, feeling a little sheepish about what had happened the night before, but eagerly anticipating our next date at his house on Rifle Camp Road. Unable to concentrate on anything at school, except which T-shirt and jeans I'd wear that night, I couldn't wait for the day to be over. On the cafeteria line at lunch, David asked me if I wanted to watch an ABC "Movie of the Week" together that night on TV, but I said I couldn't. I was going over to Kenneth's. "Oh," he said, quite dejectedly. "Him."

It seemed eighth period would never come that day, but it did. At home, after school, I finished my homework at breakneck speed and ate supper without saying very much to Marian or Frank Senior. Then I took a shower. Through the bathroom door I could hear Marian say to my father: "Why does he need to take two showers in one day? He's going to wear out his skin." When I was dressed, I waited in my bedroom for Kenneth's horn honk, which would mean he was outside waiting to take me to his house. I would have driven myself, but my driving test wasn't until the following week.

It didn't take long for things to heat up once we were on Kenneth's bed with the door locked. With the stereo set on rock-and-roll radio, we kissed and tongued each other. Then I gently bit Kenneth's throat, which, as it turned out, was his G-spot. He let out a sigh as I worked his neck. I could feel him grow hard against my leg, his penis straining to break free of his baby-blue bikini briefs and his 501s. Then, figuring it was too late to turn back now, I reached down and grabbed one big denim handful of cock. It held all the promise of what I'd felt in Van's room more than a decade earlier, but this time I wasn't going to be interrupted.

I had to have it all. So, with Kenneth's parents downstairs watching TV, I undid the buttons of his 501s, spread open the fly, and eased down the waistband of his shorts until the entire length of him sprang free. Holding it at the base with one hand, taking care not to scratch him with my teeth, I took as much of him as I could, testing my gag reflexes and straining my jaw. Whatever I was doing, I was doing it right, for soon I heard a deep moan and felt three spasms against my lower lip as three hot spurts hit the back of my throat. It was like nectar from a gun. And, with him still in my mouth, my cock pressed to his calf, I came, too, writhing against him.

At that moment, both of us deliciously spent and sticky, we heard Fred Schneider shout "Six-oh-six-oh-eight-four-two!" on the radio. WNEW was playing "6060-842" from the first B-52s album, a song about phone sex. We burst out laughing. I slid up the bed, so our faces were pressed together, and we kissed, sharing the taste of Kenneth on our tongues as we lay wrapped in each other's arms. That night, I developed an unflagging kinship with that band. Even today, when I see that yellow album cover, I think: *Fellatio!*

We didn't get caught, thank heaven. I was ecstatic.

My oral gratification was short-lived, lasting only until lunch the following day at our usual round table in the corner of the PV cafeteria. When I asked Kenneth when we were getting together that night, he said, "We're not." "We're not? Why?" I asked, instantly developing a lump in my throat and wondering exactly what I'd done wrong. "We're just not," he said, and got up and left, throwing most of his uneaten lunch in the trash can nearby.

That night, on the phone, I pressed him for an explanation of his sudden retreat, but he didn't have one. He just said we could never have sex again. He was like the little boy who vows never to masturbate again after he ejaculates for the first time—the classic "Oh-my-God-I-broke-the-thing!" reaction. "But didn't you like it?" I asked. "Yeah, but . . . look I don't want to talk about it. I've got to go," he said. With that, he put down the phone.

I was crushed that night, cut off too soon from my supply of happiness. The following day, after he'd thought about all that had happened, Kenneth told me we would be just friends, that it would be better that way. But for whom? I wondered. Certainly not for me. But, as far as Kenneth was concerned, that was that, and he was stubborn.

Of course, friendship wasn't enough for me. Once I'd had a taste, I wanted the whole gory enchilada. But I agreed to his terms, because a little Kenneth was better than none at all. For several months, I tried to be just friends, but my infatuation with him made it impossible. That winter, we had an argument that began over something incredibly stupid like who was cooler, the Sex Pistols or the Ramones, and we stopped speaking. We didn't exchange a word. Not in calculus. Not in advanced placement English. Not on the phone. Not anywhere.

In his absence, I struck up my friendship with David again, and busied myself applying to college. After doing a computer search in the guidance counselor's office, I set my sights on Northwestern University in Evanston, Illinois, eight hundred miles away from everything and everyone I knew, including Kenneth. He planned to go to Cornell to study math and science. I planned a combined major in journalism and theater, both of which Northwestern was known for. Really, though, I chose that school because Paul Lynde had gone there. I felt, after my success in *Bye Bye Birdie*, that that was where I belonged.

It was fate set to a score by Lee Adams and Charles Strouse.

Still, I missed Kenneth something awful. For one moment, I'd been happy, experiencing life with an intensity I'd never felt before, and then it was gone. As the winter months went by, I became more and more depressed, melodramatically so. My mother kept asking me what was wrong.

"You can tell me anything," she said.

No, I can't, I thought.

Finally, teenaged crazy and desperate for love, I told Marian one night on the porch, after my father had gone to bed and the TV was shut off, that the reason I was depressed was because I was hopelessly in love with Kenneth, but he wasn't in love with me. "You *have* to help me get him back," I said.

As it turned out, that wasn't one of the things I could tell her.

Her face got hard, like it always did when she heard something she didn't like. She folded her paper, pushed down the footrest of her recliner, and then stood up. Looking at me coldly for the first time ever, she said one thing and one thing only: "Just don't tell your father."

Then, in early April, three months after we'd

stopped speaking, I found an envelope in my locker with my name on the front in Kenneth's unmistakably neat handwriting. Making sure no one was around to look over my shoulder, I tore it open. Inside was a wallet-sized senior class portrait of the boy I loved— his hair center parted, him all teeth and a borrowed suit. Moving close and holding it inside my locker so no one could see, I turned it over. On the back, Kenneth had written in ballpoint: "I've loved you in a way I've never loved before. I'll cherish everything you've given me. Most of all, I'll miss the talks and therapy sessions. Hope you will think of me at college like I'll be missing you. Sartre found my number one fault. I'm sorry. I love you still and always, Kenneth."

Now, I don't know what Sartre found, but *I* found Kenneth's phone number in my hot pink telephone book with the bubble drawing of a candlestick phone on the cover and called it.

Finally, that "ghoul" was mine.

That
"Ghoul"

Good
Girls
Don't,
but Frank
Does

*T*here are lovers and
there are lovees. And in the relationship that developed
between Kenneth and me after I got his mash note
and called him, he was the lovee, upon whom I show-
ered my affections. My handsome, withholding Ghoul
Friday adored me, to be sure. But he had trouble de-
claring his affection, no matter how much time we
spent together. He was like my father in that way,
which is why I loved him so much. Kenneth became
a salve for the wounds of growing up in Little Falls.
Through him, I thought I could make up for the hurt
I'd felt at the hands of kids like Chooch and for the
emotional shortchanging I thought I'd received from
the first man in my life, Frank Senior. Of course, I
didn't look at it that way then. That spring and summer, I just looked at my relationship with Kenneth as

A
B o y
N a m e d
P h y l l i s

My One Great Forever Love Affair. We were *the* couple of the class of 1980.

At least, I thought so.

Kenneth and I didn't think of ourselves as homosexuals then, even when we were contorting ourselves on the front seat of his father's Fairmont in his driveway long after his parents had gone to bed. We were just two boys in love. Hiding our lust from our parents, we had sex every night with all the abandon of teenaged hooligans. We were insatiable for the newness of it all, our enthusiasm sugar-fueled by a diet of Entenmann's baked goods eaten at all hours. Sitting in Eleanor's breakfast nook late at night, we played footsy under the table between bites of Pecan Danish Ring, suggestively fingering the knob on his mother's lazy Susan as we looked into each other's eyes and flirted like the schoolkids-with-crushes that we were.

We had no gay identity then, no sense of a gay community existing beyond the world we knew in Little Falls—although there *was* one night when we went to Korvette's and bought copies of the English singer Tom Robinson's *Power in the Darkness* album. It had a song on it called "Glad to Be Gay," and Kenneth and I *were* glad to be gay if it meant we could have each other. But how scared we were approaching the checkout counter, my copy clutched to my chest, Kenneth's held limply at his side. Like abused children, ashamed of what we were doing, we avoided eye contact with the frizzy-haired salesgirl as she rang us up, hoping she wouldn't see the clenched fist and the words "Including Bonus L.P. Featuring 'Glad to Be Gay'" on the cover. You'd think we were buying kiddy porn at a church rummage sale. We were so frightened someone would see us and know the truth, that we were lovers, like every other teenaged couple at the mall.

Even when we took the 191 bus into the city, we didn't seek out gay life. That first time, a rainy weekday in June, we walked around the East Village, pants wet from the knees down, feet soaked, searching record stores for punk vinyl we couldn't find at Harmony Hut. We went, damp but happy, for lunch at McSorley's downing Guinness Stout and nibbling sandwiches with too-hot mustard on them. All the while, we butched it up as well as we could to make sure no one would suspect we were boyfriends. On the steps of Cooper Union after lunch, while it continued to pour, Ken tried to teach me to smoke Marlboros. Whenever I inhaled, I turned green. I was green in so many ways, but eagerly making up for lost time.

Everything seemed so alive that spring and summer. We spent them (and ourselves) love-drunk and listening to Neil Young's *Rust Never Sleeps* and Blondie's *Parallel Lines* albums on Kenneth's Kenwood. I traded Smedley and Sasquatch for two of Kenneth's friends, Lisa and "Biggs," two cool Jewish girls from Totowa. They rounded out our table at the Versailles and did our makeup for *Rocky Horror*. They knew we were a

Good
Girls
Don't,
but Frank
Does

185

couple. But even though both Lisa and Biggs were as in love with Kenneth as I was, they didn't care that he was mine. Or, if they did resent it, they never let on. In those days, it seemed that *everyone* loved Kenneth, except of course his mother and father . . . and *my* mother and father, who knew—without knowing —that, thanks to him, life on Prospect Street would never be the same.

My romance with Kenneth turned me into a more typical teenager. Under his influence, I became more rebellious, staying out till all hours, worrying my parents, who didn't always know my whereabouts, and, once in a while, although not too often, coming home drunk from too many shots of Southern Comfort swigged in a finished basement somewhere in Totowa. One thing was certain: I was a nerd no more.

When it came time for the prom in May, Kenneth and I never entertained the notion of going together as a couple. It never dawned on us that such a thing was possible. At that point in our lives, the idea of two men slow-dancing together—*even in a gay bar*— seemed alien. Instead, we were satisfied with the prospect of sitting at the same table. Kenneth asked my friend Michele, who fancied herself a Chrissie Hynde clone. For my prom date, I asked Susan, who I thought was lovers with Grace, though it turns out she wasn't. They were both really butch—the kind of young women my father would refer to as "real big jobs"—but they were very fun, especially Susan. I asked her by saying, "If I were to ask you to the prom, would you say yes?" And she said, "Yeah, I'd say yes," with a lisp that if anyone ever made mention of, she'd coldcock them. So, assured that she'd go with me, I said, "So do you want to go to the prom?" and she said yes again. I so lacked confidence when it came to girls that I almost didn't believe her. But Susan showed up and was a good date. She knew I didn't want anything off her, even though she didn't know about Kenneth. Yet.

I wore a black single-breasted tuxedo to the prom, with oversized tortoise aviator glasses with a gradient tint that went from whiskey brown at the top to clear at the bottom. These were the height of accessory chic in those days. At least to my mind. Ken's tuxedo was dove gray and double-breasted. For weeks after, I would tease him with an old elephant joke: "What's gray and comes in quarts? Ken in a tuxedo!"

That night, my mother and father took our pictures with a black plastic Kodak camera that took 126 film. We stood in front of my grandmother's prize rose-bushes. Nana came out in one of her muumuus to inspect the pre-prom festivities. After giving her little Frankie a kiss, she saw Kenneth, all dolled up, and gave him a big hug, four feet of her looking up to six feet of him. "I *like* you," she said with all the warmth of church candles on Christmas. Then, she hobbled over to David, who tagged along that night much to Kenneth's dismay, looked him square in the eye, and

said, "I *don't* like you." He wilted faster than the car-
nation on the lapel of his beige tuxedo, right in front
of his date, a short, unpleasant, emaciated girl named
Karen, who was acting as if she were doing David a
favor by being there.

I didn't know what to say, after Nana's tart-
tongued pronouncement, so I hustled everyone into
my father's midnight-blue 1970 Cadillac Coupe de
Ville, which he'd reluctantly lent me for the evening.
Beeping the horn and waving to Marian and Frank
Senior and, over the fence, to Jack and Vivian, we left
for the banquet hall on Route 17, chattering all the
way. We were quite a group, but we fit right in with
the sea of wrist corsages and mismatched rental tuxes
that awaited us. The theme of our prom was "The
Way We Were." And were we ever! Festooned with
crepe-paper ribbons, our table looked like a convention of teenagers of nebulous sexual orientation.

A cynical sextet, we expected little from any event
connected with Passaic Valley. In fact, we thought the
prom would suck. But much to our surprise we had
fun that night, eating our prime rib dinners and dancing to a band that favored Beatles covers. For once, I
was among my classmates and didn't hear the word
"fag" used about me or anyone else. We marveled at
how enjoyable it all was. After they played a version
of Donna Summer's "Last Dance"—sending Smedley
into disco orbit—we grabbed our souvenir crystal beer
steins with "The Way We Were" etched on them and

made our way to the door. We had to be up early the next morning, but we couldn't stop partying. At midnight, we parked the car at the country club next door to Kenneth's house, opened all the doors, and danced in the parking lot to "Funky Town" on the car stereo.

That was the best part of the prom. We all agreed.

The next day was traditionally senior cut day. So, with our parents turning blind eyes, we all skipped school and headed down the shore in Susan's van to Island Beach State Park. We took pictures, tanning in our cutoff shorts and tie-dyed shirts. We had lunch and we had fun, but what we didn't have, although Kenneth and I wanted it desperately, was a moment alone. We hadn't so much as kissed in twenty-four hours, which was torture for both of us. We were horny beyond belief, with no relief in sight for our teenaged lust. Finally, on the way home, as we drove up the Garden State Parkway, Kenneth and I could stand it no longer. We fell into each other's arms and held each other all the way home.

No one said a word, not even our dates.

It felt so good and so bold to be showing our affection for one another out in the open like that. We didn't do it to make a statement. We were just two young people in love at a time when the world seemed to be becoming more welcoming to gay people . . . and we wanted to share our love with the world. After all, the late seventies were a time when celebrities would say things like "To be truly liberal, you must

Good
Girls
Don't,
but Frank
Does

189

be bisexual" and rock stars bragged about having had homosexual affairs. It was also a time before AIDS, an era when *not* swallowing was considered just bad taste. Kenneth and I were thrilled to be gay. It was one more thing that separated us from our surroundings, something that got us out of Little Falls, which was our sole mission in life at that point.

Flush with my success in several Masque & Sandal productions after *Bye Bye Birdie*—I had featured roles in *Pinocchio* at Christmas and *The Fantasticks* that spring—and delirious from the fun I was having with Kenneth, I was riding high as the school year ended. I was named valedictorian, much to my parents' boastful delight and Smedley's jealous dismay. He'd been named the teachers' choice for outstanding student of the year, a sort of runner-up distinction. We both got to speak at graduation, though. On that day, in our green robes, we filed into the stadium, where the mighty Hornets usually played, and with sweaty palms sat through opening remarks waiting for our turn at the mike. Smedley spoke before I did, and his speech, delivered in a nasal whine, was a disaster, so earnest and boring we all stopped listening. Kids began to heckle. Even on graduation day, David was humiliated. I felt awful for him, but it gave me courage. Knowing I had to do something to get their attention back, I took the podium and looked out over the crowd. But instead of beginning, "Welcome friends, parents, faculty . . . ," I said, in my best Paul Lynde voice, "I've got a wonderful wife, two swell kids, a good job and now this . . ." and let out one of his signature snickers. It was my big laugh-getter from *Bye Bye Birdie* and it worked here, too. The crowd went wild. And, after a speech in which I thanked God for the friends and "lovers" I'd known at Passaic Valley —I was pretty cocky in my choice of words—my Summer of Love officially began.

The running gag that summer, as we listened to the *Get the Knack* album at Kenneth's house, was "Good girls don't, but Frank does." And I did. A lot. Never anal sex, though. I could talk Kenneth into a lot of things, but for some reason sodomy wasn't one of them. He thought it was dirty. And I didn't really mind. I was quite content with all that we *were* doing. It was a good thing Kenneth's parents played golf and socialized with other couples. We would never have had sex otherwise. We couldn't do it at my house, because at least one of my parents was always home, except when they went to mass together on Saturday night so they wouldn't have to go Sunday morning. Kenneth's parents were *never* home, and their neglect of their son ended up a boon for our relationship. We had sex there all the time. In his bed under the black-light Yes posters; on the sculptured-pile-covered stairs while Pierre, his mother's one-eared poodle, watched; and in the backyard aboveground swimming pool, in a drunken stupor brought on by too-strong Long Island iced teas that I'd mixed. This was during the day, while the family next door barbecued hamburgers and hot dogs for their relatives. That was the most exhibitionistically daring fun we had.

That summer, Kenneth began calling me by a name that would stick like glue, well into my adulthood. Kenneth starting calling me "Phyllis." He'd read in a gossip column in the *Daily News* that Elton John's friend Rod Stewart called him by that girly nickname. Not to be outdone, Elton dubbed Rod "Sharon," which is what I started calling Kenneth. In the paper, it said that Rod had hung a huge sign at Elton's most recent concert: "Phyllis, Blondes Have More Fun, Sharon." At Rod's next concert, Elton retaliated by hanging an even bigger banner that read, "Yes, Sharon, But Brunettes Have Lots More Money!" I always loved that story.

Years later, reading a biography of Elton John, I learned that Kenneth had gotten his wires crossed. Rod's nickname is Phyllis, Elton's is Sharon. But by then, it was too late for me to do anything about it. The "Phylth from Phyllis" stationery was already printed, the "Las Vegas Phyllis" mug already in my cupboard, the "Phyllis' butts" ashtray already on my desk. When I learned that, I called Kenneth, who was living in Washington, D.C., with his boyfriend of many years, and said, "You bastard! If you'd gotten it right, *I* could be living in a gorgeous townhouse with my lover and *you* could be single and living in an expensive shithole in New York." We laughed and reminisced about our Phyllis and Sharon days and about just how much more bearable we'd made life in Little Falls for each other that summer.

Two young gay people never had it better there.

At that time, we began to frequent a bar called Charlie's West in a rundown neighborhood in East Orange. It had drag shows that were so bad, they were fabulous. "Mimi," a homely blond who never tucked herself enough to complete the illusion, was always the hostess. She would lip-synch in a tricolor sequined gown—red, white, and green, like the Italian flag— and always end with "Where the Boys Are." When she got to the line "Till he holds me, I'll wait impatiently," she would make the up-and-down gesture that universally means masturbation. That was her trademark. Donny Osmond had purple socks; Carol Burnett tugged her ear; Mimi jerked off to Connie Francis. We loved Mimi and wrote her fan letters, but they always went unanswered. I asked Heidi, whom I still saw occasionally, to come with us one night, but she said, "Take my mother instead." So we did. Lois was curious and wanted to see what a gay bar was like. I'd told her about Kenneth and she didn't flinch. When I went to pick Lois up, she appeared in a blond wig, her face painted to the hilt. She was quite a hit at Charlie's. One man, though, badly dressed and a little drunk, took one look at Lois, leaned over, and whispered in my ear: "Kid, is that your father?"

I only wish it had been. That night, my parents were where they always were—at home watching TV—my mother with her feet up in the BarcaLounger, a newspaper in her lap, my father asleep on the couch, snoring away until the Channel 5 newsman said "It's ten P.M., do you know where your children are?" which meant it was time for him to go to bed.

Our summer together fled quickly. At the end of August, Kenneth left for Cornell. The following month, I would be off to Northwestern. On our last night together, I tried to be brave in my own melodramatic way. Standing on the front porch of my house—with the porch light and the post lamp turned off on purpose—I put my arms around Kenneth's faraway neck and kissed him good-bye.

"Now go off and sow your wild oats," I said to him. "If we're meant to be together, we will be."

I have since learned *never* to say this to a gay man. By Thanksgiving, he had a new boyfriend. And I had my father to deal with.

hen I was a little kid and my mother would bake my father a birthday cake or buy him a present, she'd say, "Don't tell your father. I want to surprise him." And I wouldn't breathe a word . . . until he got home from work and opened the front door and put one Florsheim down on the black-and-white linoleum in the foyer. Then, before he could even hang up his navy quilted hunting jacket in the front hall closet, I'd blurt out: "Guess what Mom baked for you . . . a cake!" or "Wait until you smell the new bottle of Hai Karate we got for you on sale at Two Guys!" I couldn't control myself. The urge to spill the beans and let him in on the scoop was just too strong.

It was the same when I told him I was gay. Well, sort of. My mother had said, "Don't tell your father," when I told her I was in love with Kenneth. But by the time I'd packed my bags and left for Northwestern, I couldn't *not* tell my father. I'd already told everyone else, including my high school advanced placement English teacher because senior year she'd given me an A on an anti–Anita Bryant composition I'd written called "Freedom for a Different Brother." I figured she'd understand about Kenneth and me. And she did. But not everyone was as open-minded as Miss Nowak. A friend of Kenneth's mother had been gossiping about us all over Little Falls that summer. Not that Kenneth and I cared very much. We knew that when we left for college, we weren't *ever* coming back to live in Little Falls.

But for all the gossip and all my not-so-subtle hints, my father's eyes were closed to the obvious. He knew *something* was up between Kenneth and me, asking more than once that summer, "What sort of spell does that kid have over you?" But he never imagined it was full-blown homosexual love. Still, Frank Senior always seemed jealous of the relationship I'd forged with Kenneth, envious that I told Kenneth things I wouldn't tell anyone else. "You always go running to him," my father would say. And, it was true. Kenneth had become the main man in my life; my father was brushed off to the side. That didn't sit well with him. He felt jilted. It was not an uncommon reaction.

When fathers find out their sons are gay, they first turn green with nausea (especially if you tell them you think fellatio is man's work) and then green with envy. First they say they never would have known; then they realize their sons have other men in their lives who are more important to them than their dear old dads are. They hate that. Mothers are the opposite. They know their sons are gay from the time they're children and, once they get over the probably-no-grandchildren thing, they're secretly glad. My mother prayed that I wouldn't turn out like her hairdressing partners. But in the long run, she was comforted by the fact that I was gay. Like every well-meaning but overly possessive mother, she knew that my gayness meant she was going to be the number one woman in my life *forever*. Lovers would come and go, but Marian would always be my Marian. She liked that idea.

Nine months after I came out to her—the day she said, "Now I'll have to put my face in shit!" (whatever that means) and the day her "You can tell me anything" offer expired (temporarily)—I decided it was time to let Frank Senior in on my not-so-secret secret. I'd just started college and was feeling empowered by the newfound independence I was enjoying. I'd only been gone a couple of months, but already I'd fallen in with a clique of gay boys from the theater department. We were our own United Nations, looking like a Benetton ad before there were Benetton ads. James was Chinese, but spoke bad Italian. Harry was a Southern gentleman, but channeled Sophie Tucker after only one vodka stinger. Denis was Irish and looked

A
B o y
N a m e d
P h y l l i s

like an altar boy. Tim was Bette Midler's cosmic twin, a Jew from Honolulu. Derwood seemed destined to play the lead in the all-black version of *Evita*. I was the Italian Catholic Rhoda Morgenstern—a New Yorker through and through, even if I was a native only by virtue of my prenatal tumorhood.

We formed a support system during those first few months away from home, helping one another through the pressures of academic life, the challenge of living without Mom and Dad looking over our shoulders, and the realization that our sex lives still left much to be desired, no matter how hard we looked for Mr. Right. We bonded freely in those days. If you liked the same Bette Midler album—*Live at Last*—you had enough in common with someone to make friends. We coupled not with each other but with others who crossed our collective path. Well, a couple of us did sleep with Derwood, our Alvin Ailey Evita. He was so scrumptious, we couldn't resist.

Between my eighteenth birthday on November 6, 1980, and Thanksgiving of that year, I decided to reach out and really touch my father by telling him over the telephone that I was gay. I wanted him to hear it from me, not from a neighborhood gossip and not from my mother. Telling him seemed the right thing to do at the time, the only course of action if I wanted him to remain in my life. My naïve plan was to tell him early in the month, so that by Thanksgiving he'd be over it and everything would be okay. We could sit down to the crucified turkey my mother always prepared and be one small happy family. Needless to say, my sense of timing was off by about fifteen years.

Still, considering how awful my father could have been when I told him I was gay, he was terrific. On the other hand, he was terrible, considering how understanding he could have been. He was terrific in that he didn't disown me and tell all our relatives "*Nostro figlio è morto*"—"Our son is dead"—or withhold my college tuition payments and make me go work in Atlantic City with cousin Danny the pit boss with the taupe shoes, or send me in for that kind of antigay therapy where they show you pictures of art deco apartments and play Barbara Cook records and then shock you with a cattle prod. He was terrible in just how melodramatic he was. "You mean all those kids were right all those years!" he said. And then, later, in a fit of Dewar's-fueled anger: "If I'd known you were going to be like this, I would have killed you at birth."

His first remark cut through me like broken glass. He'd never done much to protect me from the kids who made my school life a living hell. All he ever did was get mad at me for not fighting back. Now it seemed he was joining my tormentors' ranks, doing to me what they'd always done. His second remark, his threat, scared the living daylights out of me, even though in retrospect I should have known he was just ranting. Thank heaven I wasn't born into what my father called the real *ginzo* part of our family tree, where the sap was strictly Progresso. That Thanksgiving, I might have ended up like someone in a Mario Puzo novel, an ice pick jabbed right through me into our breakfront, a dead teen queen in a pile of Stove Top stuffing, Ocean Spray cranberry sauce, and broken Lenox china.

Still, even without such full-scale theatrics, my coming-out process was an awful lot of fuss and heartache for something that, in truth, was no great revelation. I'm glad Marian and Frank weren't too understanding, though. Parents who offer too much understanding—something I did *not* have to worry about—deprive their gay children of something very special. As upset as I was, I felt really important causing such a ruckus just for being me. It gave me a sense of power over them. Neither of my parents ever asked me, "Are you sure you're gay?" They believed me from the get-go. Their reaction was more like, "Yeah, you are. Now what the hell are we supposed to do about it?" If I'd been more conservative, I suppose, they might have handled it better. Clearly, Marian and Frank Senior weren't prepared for a son whose ideas about homosexuality were grandiose. Even then I believed that if you're going to be gay, you might as well be fabulous.

Leopard print for day! That was my rallying cry.

When I came out, I realized that being gay was something I was good at, something at which I could excel. No wonder I was so bad at being a heterosexual: I *wasn't* one! Like the girl in *The Fantasticks* who says "Please, God, please, don't let me be normal," I was happy that my gayness made me officially and unequivocally different.

That, my parents *really* didn't understand.

What happened between the Franks, Senior and Junior, in the days after I told my parents I was gay was not good. My disclosure widened the already gaping rift between us. That first year of college, we fought whenever we spoke about the subject of homosexuality—which was just about every phone call. "It's bad enough you're this way, but why do you have to tell people? *Why must your life be an open book?*" Frank Senior would say, making me feel like a tremendous disappointment.

As my father saw it, my gayness should remain a deep dark secret. He didn't buy my argument that it was something to be proud of, something vital that made me the person I truly was. To me, my sexual orientation was a godsend, one more way to feel separate from my family and a background of which I was increasingly ashamed. At Northwestern, I mixed with rich kids for the first time. My upbringing—not to mention my wardrobe—seemed tacky compared to theirs. Truly, when your dorm roommate tells you his father tried to buy the Philadelphia Phillies, and the most expensive thing your father ever bought was a used 1970 Coupe de Ville, you feel a little outclassed, even if the car did have power windows. I wanted to be rich.

To retaliate against my father for his anger, I went out of my way to make him feel stupid and to prove to him that college—even two months' worth—had changed me. I shook off my Italian Catholic working-class roots right there in front of him on my mother's mauve sculptured carpet, and he wasn't happy about it. From then on, he knew I didn't want to live in his world, and nothing he could offer me would ever be good enough again. I redefined "haughty" right there on Prospect Street, in the white house with the Blessed Virgin Mary in the bathtub out front.

"You don't belong in Bloomingdale's," he taunted me when I left to go shopping one night. But I was out to show him I *did* belong there, and at Northwestern, and in Manhattan. And that the only place I *didn't* belong was Little Falls. I decided that if I wasn't the son he'd bargained for, then he and my mother weren't the parents I wanted to call my own. I wanted to come home from college to Thurston and Lovey Howell, the filthy-rich stuffed shirt and his delightfully dotty (and terribly chic) wife on *Gilligan's Island.* Instead, the Italian-American Archie and Edith Bunker always met me at Gate E-12 at Newark International Airport.

Before that first Thanksgiving home even got under way there was trouble. Having just flown in from Chicago, I spotted a handsome man—my gaydar was now up and running—at baggage claim, and began to flirt with him. I walked in front of him, sexily I thought, and gave him the eye. My father, suspicious of my every move, caught me in mid-cruise. In the car on the way home, he yelled at me for being so obvious. "What the hell were you strutting for? You want everyone to know?" Frank was livid, but I was glad. I'd felt so rejected by him for so many years that I began to enjoy rejecting him back.

Our worst argument over my sexuality resulted in a near tragedy. It was the first summer I was home. Frank Senior got so angry with me that he began to drink. When the Dewar's hit his blood-pressure pill, he passed out in the middle of a tirade in the foyer and put his head through the glass in the storm door. I drove him to the emergency room and waited for him to get stitches. Then I joined Kenneth and Michele at a Duran Duran/Blondie concert at the Meadowlands. I missed David Johansen, the warm-up act, thanks to my father's episode, and I was mad.

But I was also feeling guilty because I knew how much I'd hurt him.

It wouldn't be the last time we hurt each other. For years I made it clear to him, by rejecting everything he stood for, that he was *not* my hero. I could no longer see the goodness in his heart or the reasons we'd nicknamed him St. Francis when I was a kid. It would be years before we became close again, and by that point, neither of us thought that day would ever come.

There seemed little hope of a reconciliation in 1980 or '81.

Even ten years after that, Frank Senior wouldn't really understand my inability to be anything but openly gay, or my desire to tell not only him and my mother, but the world, *everything*. He didn't know that public confession, to use a Catholic term, was my way of making sense of things. That I needed to share my innermost thoughts and all my secrets, or else I couldn't live with them—not in peace, anyway. Frank Senior will never really understand his son's life. And he will probably never apologize—not in so many words, anyway—for the ugly things he'd said when I told him I was gay. But then, I have never understood his life either, or said I was sorry for all that I'd said in return. It turns out my father and I are a lot alike in that way—both self-centered, both believing we were always right; each unable to say "I love you" even though we both knew it was mutual and true.

The fruit *didn't* fall far from the tree after all.

"There was a time there when you didn't like us very much," my mother said to me one day years later, sitting in her recliner in the room we still called the porch. It was shortly before my thirtieth birthday. By then, I'd been living in New York for four years and had just begun writing an openly gay humor column for the tabloid *New York Newsday*. She was in her seventies, still chubby and cute, her hair more salt than pepper but still teased like it had always been since the days when it was red and so was her temperament.

"You didn't like me much, either," I replied.

"*Your father* didn't like you," Marian said, resigned but sounding slightly wistful about the time and love that had been lost between the two men in her life over the years. "I *always* liked you."

Coming
Out

Together Again for the Very First Time

There is a downside to thinking everything is about you: it's thinking everything is your fault. I know this all too well. In 1980, less than a year after I came out and just after I left for college, my mother was diagnosed as clinically depressed. I was eighteen years old and eight hundred miles away, following my dream of being an actor, journalist, and major homosexual, running around Chicago in my old yellow-piped, pointy-toed Giorgio Brutini lace-ups with an army of theater-department gay boys.

Naturally, given my nature, I assumed I was solely to blame for Marian's condition. Forget that Frank Senior, to whom she'd been happily married for nearly thirty years, was forced to choose that year between quadruple bypass surgery and certain death, his con-

207

dition complicated by the heart attack he'd suffered when I was a baby. And forget that by that time Nana, who had single-handedly spiced up our lives on Prospect Street with her Pabst Blue Ribbon feistiness, had developed advanced Alzheimer's disease. She was incontinent and barely able to walk, and no longer recognized any of us. Marian tried to care for her mother, but when it proved too much, was forced to put her in a nursing home, something she'd hoped she'd never have to do. No, despite all this, my mother's depression was all my gay fault.

An ax wouldn't have done a better job of killing her.

For years, I felt I was the *only* reason that my mother spent much of the 1980s sitting silently in her brown-vinyl-covered BarcaLounger and refusing to leave the house except to go to church. She would sit for hours and stare out the window into the nothingness beyond the neighborhood treeline, the chestnuts and elms over the top of Vera's house. My mother did just that every day for nearly a decade. Thanks to me. Or so I believed.

Then, in 1990, she tried Prozac, which was the best thing that ever happened to her. Not because the so-called wonder drug worked. Marian *hated* taking it, and did so for only about a month. It was the best thing because trying Prozac got my mother to stop taking the *other* mood-altering pill she'd been misprescribed in—that's right—1980, the pill that was more to blame for her sad, sleepy condition than her openly gay son, her ailing husband, and her senile mother combined.

I told my Kenneth, who was by then an epidemiologist, what drug my mother had been on all those years, unbeknownst to any of us. He said, "That quack of a doctor had her on horse tranquilizers! No wonder she didn't want to get out of her chair. She couldn't! Don't you dare let her go back on them!" I followed his advice, and so did she. After all those years, my knight in plaid flannel really had come to the rescue.

Marian never did go back on those pills, or any others. She didn't need to. Without them she was reborn. As I settled into my thirties, she became as funny and zestful as she'd been when I was a kid, when she'd paint me ceramic motorcycle boys with eyes like Keane paintings, and send me Santa Claus cards that read, "It's Christmastime and you know what that means . . . Numb nuts rides again!" After a decade of depression, my mother was back and intent on making up for lost time. My father, comfortable in retirement, could barely keep up with her renewed vigor.

In her seventies, Marian became more gay-positive than I could ever have imagined, and while Little Falls seemed to stay the same, she moved forward. At Holy Angels on my thirtieth and her seventy-third Christmas Eve, I leaned over to her in the blond-wood pew we shared with her girlfriend Rose and said, "What would these priests say if they knew I hadn't been to confession in fifteen years?"

"Oh, they won't mind," my mother shot back. "What do you think, they're not queer?" And then she giggled, amused at her boldness and a little self-surprised, as if she were wondering where exactly those words came from. But I knew. I'd seen this woman before. This was the woman who had said to me, "You can tell me anything," and, although she reneged for a while there, really did mean it after all. That night, I knew it would only be a matter of time before we would be as close as we had been all those years ago —my little pear-shaped bundle of Aqua Net and her not-so-little Frankie.

I convinced my mother the following year that it would be a good idea if she came out to her best girlfriend about me. I'd been urging her to tell for years, saying that Rose already suspected something was up because men in their thirties who have a dozen women friends and no girlfriend usually are big you-know-whats. Besides, I said, I know Rose knows because when my friend Dan and I visited her, she asked us if we wanted to buy her house and nothing on her face said "bachelor pad."

"Marian, she thought we were a couple," I said.

Anyway, sixteen years after I came out to my mother, she took Rose out for manicotti in a strip-mall restaurant in West Paterson where the two of them were regulars, and broke the news to her. "There's something I have to tell you," my mother said. "My dear, sweet son, of whom I'm very proud"—she laid it on thicker than Polly-O ricotta—"is gay."

"I know," Rose said, "I read it in *New York* magazine."

Well, so much for Marian Teresa LaRegina De-Caro's big homo bombshell. Rose's son, who's straight, had sent her a clipping of a *New York* "Intelligencer" item that called me an "avowedly gay" writer. The boldface publicity came as no shock to Rose. It only confirmed what she had thought for at least several years.

"Do you think less of Frankie?" my mother asked.

"Why would I think less of him? I adore him," she replied.

Rose reacted exactly as I thought she would. She'd always had one of the biggest hearts in the neighborhood—not to mention the largest collection of Capodimonte figurines. Besides, she has always prided herself on keeping up with modern life, and knowing openly gay and lesbian people is part of that. She handled it perfectly.

This little interchange between two seventysomething women in hand-painted sweatshirts and sensible shoes—this scene from an Italian restaurant—was a turning point in their relationship and a great leap forward in their relationships with me. It was as if a huge weight had been lifted off my mother's shoulders, and a lesser one off mine. Finally, after so many years, one of her peers told my mother it's not her fault that her son is gay, that sexual orientation isn't good or bad, it just *is*. Marian needed to hear it from someone besides me. I wasn't exactly prepared for all the changes that were to follow, however, and neither was my father. Once the cards were on the table, Marian and Rose became the Thelma and Louise of the Metamucil set. The summer after she came out to Rose, they left my father—Rose was a widow by then—and took a bus to the Concord in the Catskills. This was a big deal, because for years my mother would never go anywhere without my father.

Four days later they came back, and my mother reported: "I met the cutest singer. I wanted to bring him home for you, but he was engaged." She left a mother and came back Dolly Levi in stretch pants. She even began showing signs of activism. When Olympic diver Greg Louganis came out of the closet, she said, "I think it's great. If you're gonna be queer, you might as well be honest about it." "If this keeps up," I said to my friend Dan, "I'll go home one Sunday and she'll be cooking ziti for Larry Kramer."

"You know what I did yesterday?" she said one day. "I got all dressed up and left your father home doing the lawn or puttering around or whatever the hell he was doing and drove to Montclair. I went to see *Priscilla, Queen of the Desert*. I bought a big Diet Coke and sat there all by myself. It was terrific."

"You went by yourself?"

"What, you think your father's going to go see a movie about drag queens? Besides, Rose was busy. I loved that young guy with the dark hair. He was so cute. Whatshisname? Can't you meet someone like that?"

"He's straight, Mother. Did you like the dress made out of flip-flops?"

"I must have missed that part. I had to go to the bathroom from all the Diet Coke. You know how it is when you're old."

Needless to say, I was delighted. My mother was entering my world, and I didn't even have to coax her anymore. Her matinee experience was not an isolated incident. When I told her I was seeing this cute shy guy around the time of my thirty-second birthday, and that I missed him a lot when I went away on business, she teased me:

"My little Phyllis is in love," she cooed.

I laughed and then turned five shades of Coco Pink. My mother had called me by my girl name! I couldn't believe my ears. I was burning with a mixture of embarrassment and delight.

"You are too much," I said.

"Well, enjoy me now," she replied, "I'm not going to be here long."

I told this story to my friend Bill, a sexually adventurous soul who redefined what it meant to be out of the closet in 1982 by wearing leather chaps to our nine A.M. continental fiction class at Northwestern. I called

Together
Again for
the Very
First
Time

213

him from JFK while I was waiting to board a plane for Milan. I was going off on assignment to the Italian fashion collections. Bill had just gotten out of the hospital—Kaposi's sarcoma and various other opportunistic infections were ravaging his thirty-two-year-old body—and he was back at home in Brooklyn. He laughed, his nasal Robby Benson voice now sounding more like Harvey Fierstein's, and said, "You'll have to enjoy me now, too."

Bill—a man who adored S&M as much as my mother loved the A&P—didn't last much longer, but he was bold right up to the end. He was pleased, I'll never forget, the day that I told him Madonna was responsible for a major breakthrough in my relationship with my father.

When her book, *Sex*, came out, I was in Paris covering the French designer collections, and was planning to leave the next day, so I phoned my father and mother the way I always do the day before I fly to say "I love you" and "I'll call you when I get home." That's so just in case the plane goes down, my final words to them weren't something like "If you see Tab on sale at ShopRite, get me a case and I'll give you the money."

Anyway, I was in my hotel room across from the Louvre, telling my father about Jean-Paul Gaultier's latest collection and about all the celebrities I'd spotted that week in the front rows of all the shows, fully knowing he didn't know who or what I was talking about, but expecting him to listen intently nonetheless, when he surprised the hell out of me.

Frank Senior asked, "Did you get Madonna's book yet?"

"No. It only came out today," I said, stunned that he'd even heard of it. "I'm going to get it tomorrow on the way home from the airport. I'll make the driver stop while I run in to Barnes & Noble. I'm dying to see it."

"She's with a dog in it, you know," he said, more amused than disgusted.

"Really? Cool."

"Oh, I figured you'd like that," he said. "Anything weird, you like."

He couldn't have said anything that would have made me happier. For once, my father was talking to me about someone and something I was interested in, acknowledging a world beyond Little Falls, the one I lived in, in fact. And, God love him, *he* brought it up. We could share something after all. I wasn't always sure we could. My father is a tough man to win over.

When I turned thirty-two, I finally did, though. After years of saying no, my father actually agreed to come to a birthday party I was throwing in my twelfth-floor one-bedroom apartment in Chelsea. "If we're feeling up to it, we'll come Saturday night," he had said. But I knew they'd show and bring Rose with them. I'd asked everyone to dress up for cocktails and hors d'oeuvres, and by the time my parents and their friend buzzed up from the lobby, my place was crawling with people. In their dressiest clothes from Meyer Brothers and Stern's, they waded into a sea of fifty-two well-dressed, successful, openly gay men and a handful of straight friends who were used to being in mostly gay situations. This was a first for my folks, not only because it was a nighttime visit—they usually come only on Sundays during the day—but because they'd never been among so many gay men. That evening meant a lot to me, because to be there, my parents had to conquer their fear of New York at night, a huge phobia that my father had nurtured since I was a kid.

Not to mention a certain other phobia he'd always seemed to have.

Putting on a CD of *Whipped Cream and Other Delights* by Herb Alpert and the Tijuana Brass, I was worried about how the Feenamint Twins and Rose would mix among the manhattans and martinis and Mary men that I'd assembled. But they did quite well, actually, splitting up and circulating through the crowd in my living room, nibbling cheese sticks, and cashews, and *crostini* with *tapenade,* then settling on the black couch near the windows to survey the situation.

"We're holding court over here," Rose said, as another group of my friends—smart people in smarter clothes—introduced themselves, fawning over my parents and her as if they were the Duke and Duchess of Windsor and guest. Gay men always treat parents like celebrities, as long as they're not *their own* parents. Rose and Marian enjoyed the attention being lavished upon them, I could tell. It was the first time in decades that men—honest-to-goodness penis-bearing members of society—had actually paid attention to them, asking them questions and really listening to their replies.

For my father, the evening was more difficult. I found him in the kitchen, drinking a seltzer and talking to Nancy, one of my women friends, upon whom he'd always had a bit of a crush. He had talked mostly to my straight female friends all night, kibitzing with them and talking about all I'd done to the apartment since I moved in—the black-and-white stripes I'd had painted in the hall, the bright yellow walls of the office, the vintage chic furniture I'd dragged home from the flea market on Twenty-sixth Street. But even if he didn't become best friends with every man in the room, he didn't do so badly himself. Just having him in that apartment with all those queens was a major accomplishment, a feat fourteen years in the making.

At nine-fifteen, although the cocktails had just kicked in and the party was in full swing, my father decided he'd had enough, as he always does when things are just starting to get good. But although he was ready, Marian wasn't. No, she was laughing and teasing my friends and talking about how tall RuPaul was, especially compared to her. My father, putting on his coat, practically had to drag my mother away from her audience and out of the apartment.

"Your father wants to go," she said to me. "But I want to meet your friend Frank, the stand-up comedian, before I leave."

"He's the cute one in the bedroom," I said.

"They're all cute. Don't worry, I'll find him."

Ten minutes later she reappeared, in her coat now, with a satisfied smile on her face. "All right, now I can go. Where's your father?"

"He's holding the elevator. He's got Rose with him."

"They can't wait a minute, can they?" Marian said, standing on her tippy-toes to give me a kiss good-bye. "I'll call you tomorrow."

And, with that, she made her exit, my former femme fatale.

The following day, Marian called, a bit too early for the hangover I was nursing, but eager to talk to me about the night before. "There were a lot of good-looking men at that party," she said. "Rose and I are old, but we still notice. You could have served some real food, though. We were so hungry when we left we had to stop at the Golden Star on the way home. I'm putting your father on. Wait a minute." She cupped her hand over the receiver, although not nearly enough to shield my ears, and screamed, "All right, you can pick it up now!"

My father got on the extension phone. "Hey, buddy, how you doing?" he said as he'd done a thousand times before.

"Oh, I'm a little hung over," I said.

"Those manhattans sneak up on you. Thanks for having me at the party last night," he said. "It was nice." After a little small talk—what presents I got, how much liquor was left over—my father said, "Your friends really like you, huh?" He was impressed, and maybe even a bit surprised. Deep down, I fear, he'd always worried I'd be lonely because I was gay.

"Yeah, I guess they do like me," I replied.

"You know," I added, "they really liked you, too."

With that, it was as if I could hear him smile.

For once, both Franks were pleased.

Together Again for the Very First Time